T0358469

ROUTLEDGE LIBRARY EDITIONS:
WOMEN AND BUSINESS

Volume 1

BECOMING A TOP WOMAN MANAGER

BECOMING A TOP
WOMAN MANAGER

LEONIE V. STILL

Routledge
Taylor & Francis Group

LONDON AND NEW YORK

First published in 1988 by Unwin Hyman

This edition first published in 2017
by Routledge
2 Park Square, Milton Park, Abingdon, Oxon OX14 4RN

and by Routledge
711 Third Avenue, New York, NY 10017

Routledge is an imprint of the Taylor & Francis Group, an informa business

British Library Cataloguing in Publication Data
A catalogue record for this book is available from the British Library

ISBN: 978-1-138-23710-0 (Set)
ISBN: 978-1-315-27106-4 (Set) (ebk)
ISBN: 978-1-138-24430-6 (Volume 1) (hbk)
ISBN: 978-1-315-27693-9 (Volume 1) (ebk)

Publisher's Note
The publisher has gone to great lengths to ensure the quality of this reprint but
points out that some imperfections in the original copies may be apparent.

Disclaimer
The publisher has made every effort to trace copyright holders and would welcome
correspondence from those they have been unable to trace.

BECOMING A TOP WOMAN MANAGER

Leonie V. Still

ALLEN & UNWIN
Sydney   Wellington   London   Boston

To my mother and father
who continue to know the real story

First published in 1988
Second impression 1990
Allen & Unwin Australia Pty Ltd
An Unwin Hyman company
8 Napier Street, North Sydney, NSW 2060 Australia

Allen & Unwin New Zealand Limited
75 Ghuznee Street, Wellington, New Zealand

Unwin Hyman Limited
15-17 Broadwick Street, London W1V 1FP England

Unwin Hyman Inc.
8 Winchester Place, Winchester, Mass 01890 USA

National Library of Australia
Cataloguing-in-Publication entry:

Still, Leonie V. (Leonie Veronica)
   Becoming a top woman manager.
   ISBN 0 04 442206 7.

   1. Women executives—Australia. 2. Women in business
   —Australia. I. Title.

658.4'09'024042

Library of Congress Catalog Card Number: 87-27061

Set in 10/12 Rockwell by Best-set Typesetter Ltd, Hong Kong
Printed in Hong Kong

Contents

Acknowledgements

THIS BOOK IS one of the outcomes of the *Women in Management Study* which was supported by research grants from the former Bureau of Labour Market Research of the Commonwealth Department of Employment and Industrial Relations and the New South Wales Institute of Technology where I was employed as an academic between January 1983 and December 1985. The research began in 1983 with two colleagues: Dr Jennifer Jones of the University of Wollongong and Ross Cameron, formerly of the New South Wales Institute of Technology and now of Hawkesbury Agricultural College. Ross left the project towards the end of 1983 because of other time-consuming commitments and Jenny left in 1984. My thanks go to them for the advice on questionnaire design during the pilot study stage and the firming up of the research methodology for the main study. Two research assistants then joined the project to assist with the distribution and collection of thousands of questionnaires and the unenviable task of coding the information for the computer. Cecily

Guerin worked tirelessly for five months in 1984 before departing for overseas, and rejoined in 1986 to assist with interviewing the women executives in the 'oral-history' study. Cindy Besley was an invaluable assistant during the latter part of 1984. Without their help and patience the material on which much of the book is based would not have been sorted into comprehensible form.

Researchers often find that help comes from unexpected quarters. I am grateful for the assistance provided by Lyn Russell, then employed in the public service in Darwin. She ensured that a true 'Australian' sample on attitudes was obtained. Serge Mukki, the Australian Institute of Management, the NSW Women and Management Group, the Victorian Women In Management Group, Woolworths Limited, the University of Wollongong and the New South Wales Institute of Technology helped either by handing out and collecting questionnaires and/or by providing 'subjects' for research data. What was even more pleasing was the general acceptance of the general public to the numerous questionnaires that were distributed by mail with several repeats as follow-ups. Instead of treating the research as 'junk' mail, many people spent considerable time to ensure that the research produced some meaningful results and were helpful with suggestions and anecdotes on experiences. Because the mail-outs were anonymous I am unable to thank the individuals personally but I was delighted by the interest shown in the project. Again, 239 Australian companies and 62 advertising agencies graciously answered rather time-consuming questionnaires regarding their employment of women managers. Knowing how organisations are inundated with surveys of various types, the response from the companies was tremendous and revealed their interest in the project.

As for the women who participated in the 'oral history' study on which much of this book is based, words cannot express sufficient thanks for their time and openness. While stories, incidents and names have been disguised (with the exception of Hinke Haisma and Dr Alessandra Pucci) to protect confidentiality, there are 'parts' of these women in the following pages—Bev Dyke, Peg Pattie, Helen Hill, Susan Horwitz, Aileen Kinnear, Marian Diesner, Val Steward, Judith Kerr, Wendy Ekstein, Vivienne Soo, Dr Sandra Humphries, Priscilla Shorne, Wendy Evans, Pauline Markwell and Gabrielle Potrykus.

Finally, I thank my mother who ensured I started writing at 5 o'clock in the morning and who supported the project with innumerable cups of tea and the reading of drafts. My father assisted by ensuring that life proceeded normally in its day-to-day operations. Without such support on the home front, this book would not have been written.

Foreword

THROUGHOUT THIS BOOK considerable mention is made of the *Women in Management Study*. This was a major Australian research study on the position of women in management which I conducted, with the assistance of two research assistants, between 1984 and 1987.

The *Women in Management Study* was launched in 1984, following a preliminary pilot study of attitudes in 1983. While emphasis was placed on the status of women managers within the business world, the position of women managers in the public, tertiary education and professional arenas was also considered. The study comprised three stages.

The first stage examined the attitudes of 1093 Australians towards women in management. The sample comprised 235 men managers, 198 women managers, 257 men and 158 women future managers (business students), and 101 men and 144 women non-managers from the general population. The main issues explored were general attitudes towards women managers, preferences for a male or a female boss and management style, and attitudes towards equal employment opportunity for women.

The second stage was a national survey of major Australian companies on the status of women managers within those organisations. Information was obtained on the incidence of women managers, their level of management, functional areas and salary levels, educational attainment and age distribution, and their training and promotion opportunities vis-a-vis male managers. A total of 239 companies (138 with and 101 without women managers) provided this information. They represented a broad cross-section of Australian firms in relation to type of industry, occupation, company ownership (Australian or overseas), classification of organisation (from partnership to public companies) and national coverage. Data was also obtained from 62 Australian advertising agencies to illustrate the situation within a particular industry.

The third stage was an 'oral history' study of the experiences of 50 women managers and entrepreneurs/small business proprietors. While many women were again from the business world, others represented the public sector and the professions. The interviews explored the career and personal histories and experiences of these women to determine strategies for action for aspiring women managers. Stage three also included a study of the career-related networking activities of 137 men and 115 women executives. These practices were examined to establish whether there were any gender differences in the way managers used support mechanisms to assist their careers. Interest centred on the methods used to seek assistance to change employment, career counselling and financial assistance; professional membership and extent of activity in this membership; and business and social entertaining practices.

Finally, the 'assertiveness' of women managers was contrasted in relation to men and women of the general population and their male counterparts in the managerial world. Lack of assertiveness is often claimed to be a reason for women's poor representation in authority positions. The assertiveness study tested this proposition and found that while women in the general population may be less assertive than men, those in the managerial world were more so than male managers.

The *Women in Management Study* thus examined a number of stereotypes and myths surrounding women in management and provided Australian evidence of the existence of these—the first study to do so. It also represents the first comprehensive examination of the position of women in management in Australia. This book does not summarise the findings: the place for those lies in the research literature. However, where appropriate to highlight a point of view, some of the findings are used in the text.

This book has primarily emerged from general impressions gained of the situation for career-oriented women during the four years of the study. A forerunner *Everything A Woman Needs to Know About Winning the Corporate Battle* (Horwitz-Grahame) was published in 1986, while a third, containing the material of the 50 'oral-history' interviews, has yet to be written. This book—the second in the trilogy —is dedicated to all those women who wish to achieve and need an occasional 'spur' to do so.

1

The route to senior management

THE GOAL

So you want to be a top woman manager? You have worked your way into management and you wish to establish yourself in a career. You have a good education, your parents have encouraged you to follow your own path, there are opportunities unlimited, and you have the energy, enthusiasm and commitment for the task ahead. In the media you see the various role models—those well-dressed women at all the important functions—or you observe them on the platforms of the conference venues speaking in well-modulated voices. You ask yourself: 'Why not me? Why can't I be the one up there? What do I have to do to reach my full potential, to reach senior management?'

Now that women are beginning to find their way into senior positions, their successes are heralded by the media with great fanfare. 'First woman this' and 'first woman that' is the catch-cry of the day. There are now women leaders of political parties, women Prime

1

Ministers, Cabinet Ministers, board members and managing directors. There are women astronauts, airline pilots and engineers. Wherever you go, women seem to be breaking new ground, and in a highly visible way. They seem to have at last come into their own. All a woman has to do is to reach out and take the opportunity.

The fact is, closer examination reveals a different story. Like it or not, women in senior management are few and far between. The reason you hear so much about the ones who are so visible is that *they are the only ones*. The percentage of women in the senior levels of Australian management varies from one to five, depending on the particular industry. It appears to be more because of the publicity that has accompanied their achievement.

This does not mean that there are not many more women currently working their way towards senior management. There are many attempting to emulate the famous few. What most do not realise, however, is that it is a long, hard road. Many fall by the wayside. Occasionally this is due to the individual's own making. More often it is because she does not know the system or game she is entering. As Harragan[1] points out, many women have not been successful because 'most of us have been playing solitaire in the middle of a football field wondering why we are being trampled to death'.

So, if you really want to be a success in management, to occupy the corner office (that symbol of success), to travel the world, sit on committees and boards, become a prominent personality surrounded by an entourage of people, then there are some fundamental issues that have to be addressed.

For instance, while you may have the desire, do you have the staying power? Are you persistent, consistent and single-minded? Are you prepared for the hard work, the dedication and commitment? Above all, are you willing to sacrifice your soul at the altar of the career in order to become one of the elite—the managerial achievers?

If yes, then you should be prepared for the climb. Any serious mountaineer can tell you that conquering the tricky peaks takes years of planning and careful thought. You should also consider whether you can sustain your desire through many trials and tribulations. Again like the mountaineer, *keep going and keep your eye on the objective*. You have to have a certain amount of tenacity and 'grit' to reach your desired goal.

THE STRATEGY

Successful achievers arrive at their destination because they usually have a long-term strategy. Sometimes this is a deliberate plan; more often it is an instinctive sense of career direction. These days sophisticated managers endeavour to emulate the achievements of their more instinctive and entrepreneurial colleagues through developing 'game-plans', 'business plans', 'marketing strategies' and 'managerial competencies'. They are assisted in these efforts by consultants and tertiary educational institutions which promote the managerial career benefits of undertaking Master of Business Administration (MBA) programmes. New 'buzz' words—such as environmental analysis, macro- and micro-analysis, and situational analysis—have been formed to familiarise executives with the task that lies ahead. Reaching a senior position is promoted as a step-by-step process, similar to launching a new product or achieving a take-over.

Until recently this step-by-step process was the exclusive province of men. However, examination of the financial pages of the more popular business-oriented magazines reveals that women are now apparently 'breaking through'. For instance, the fortnightly finance magazine *Australian Business* pictured the female chief economist of the Australian Industrial Development Corporation, Carol Austin, on the cover of a 1986 issue which featured her article 'Australia's economic myths'. Such attention would have been unheard of two years previously, let alone an organisation having a woman as its chief economist. The prominence given to Carol Austin's article demonstrated that women did understand the nuances of getting to the top and were able to address other similar achievers in the language of the 'arrived'.

However, this does not apply to all women with similar ambitions. Some believe that success just magically happens, provided they wait long enough and work hard enough; others fantasise that it will arrive overnight like a Hollywood talent scout; still others believe that the only way a woman can succeed is to marry success and ride on the coattails of her spouse. To the truly ambitious, however, the way to the top consists of a series of steps—all of which require time, patience, hard work and synchronisation with luck and fate.

If you wish to become a top woman manager you will get there much faster if you know these steps. With knowledge comes power: the power to right your career direction if you have been stationary or running around in circles.

However, if you feel you are not yet ready to become a top woman manager, or would like to delay that decision for a while, then the knowledge will not assist you. Because you do not have a strong career desire, you will not use the knowledge effectively and instinctively at the critical times.

Two crucial questions

To be successful you need to answer two key questions. The first is: what type of manager do you want to be? The truly ambitious or the late developer? The truly ambitious will learn the steps and be able to act accordingly. The late developer will still be 'arriving' in the years to come.

The second is: what do you want your career to give you? Answering this question will enable you to develop strategies to overcome the obstacles and barriers that lie ahead. The essence of career management is to be able to capitalise on opportunities. Once you know what you want, or where you are going, the direction will be clear, and you will be on your way.

THE GUIDEPOSTS

Well, what is this step-by-step process to the top in the managerial world? Analysis of the careers of many top people reveals it to comprise:

- An environmental or situational analysis: these are the latest 'buzz' words which camouflage the hard work needed to establish a base line from which to commence. Every successful managerial achiever needs a starting point by which to judge their eventual success. Most locate this point by undertaking a feasibility study or some research on the current situation. In your case, this might be determining the current situation for women managers. For instance, how many there are and the industries and occupations in which they work. Such information would provide you with an idea of the problems and opportunities that lie ahead.

- The second step is to become aware of the barriers and hurdles that may block achievement. Sometimes these barriers and hurdles are educational or physical ones. More often they are attitudinal. It is important to learn about these because they are usually entrenched in organisational cultures, making it difficult for aspiring women to overcome them.

■ The third step is to learn how to 'fit in' in order to achieve. Achievers adapt to the environment in which they find themselves so that they can use that environment. While this adaptation may involve some herculean efforts—especially if your values or temperament do not coincide with those you have to work with—it is an important ingredient for success and marks the individual out as being adaptable and flexible.

■ The fourth step is to have the right career direction. Usually this means finding your 'niche' in whatever specialty you like and then projecting your career upwards through a series of vertical steps. Achievers always go for the vertical—never the horizontal! Neither can you afford to dally along the way. The ones marked for senior positions never dawdle in jobs that merely happen to interest them nor do they detour into sidetracks.

■ The fifth step is to use the social system to assist you in your climb. This means joining various groups, making and using contacts, and generally developing a series of 'friendships' which may come in handy at the most unexpected times. Networking and contacts become the order of the day—including putting others under an obligation for future needs. While this may seem distasteful, remember that other aspiring achievers are doing it to you!

■ The sixth step is to learn from the triumphs and mistakes of others. No success story is without its problems; usually there have been many defeats before the final triumph. The experiences of others hold the key to many a successful career path.

■ Finally, the most important step is doing it yourself! Don't just think or dream success. *Do something about it.* While this may involve hard work, sacrifice and dedication, the rewards will be there in the end. It is a matter of deciding what you want to do, and then attempting to achieve it. While you may not always achieve what you desire, you will achieve something—and that something will usually be preferable to the base line you started from!

If it sounds too simple it is because these are merely the guideposts on your path to senior management. But they are guideposts used by other successful achievers. What we now have to do is fill in the detail. Should the detail become overwhelming, remember that you can easily come back to these guideposts for clarification.

2

Where are the women managers?

THE BASELINE: THE PROMISE

1976 marked the beginning of the International Decade for Women. Women as a group were promised many things. For instance, it was expected that great changes would occur in the social and employment status of women; that women now had a right to a career, not just a job; that women had a chance to improve themselves, to be recognised as individuals and to develop their talents and abilities; that women could combine marriage and a career (i.e. 'have it all'); and that women could enter management and should aim for senior positions. Numerous women's organisations were formed to assist and support ambitious women in their quest for a career. Governments created women's departments to improve the employment status of women and introduced legislation to remove discriminatory barriers. The whole socio-cultural environment seemed alive with opportunities and promises. For the ambitious woman, it seemed that the path ahead was at last clear.

6

1985 saw the end of the International Decade for Women. It was a time for re-assessment of the progress that had been made in the previous ten years. Had the promise become reality? Had women reached the top management levels? Had they gained access to different fields of management or were they confined to specific areas? Were they accepted as equal partners in terms of their contribution to the organisation?

THE BASELINE: THE REALITY

Consider these opinions from various women:

> During the 1960s and 1970s, changes took place in Australian social and legal institutions, promising women more of the rights that are accepted as appropriate for citizens of democratic countries. Even though there still remain gaps between promise and reality in many instances, achievements for women in the employment area have been substantial. (Jenni Neary, former Director of Women's Bureau, September 1985, commenting on the end of the Decade)[1]

> I have always wanted to be a ... manager. I don't know why. Perhaps it was because I have had plenty of opportunity to observe managers in action and I suppose I built up a whole range of views on good and bad management until it got to the stage where I thought I would like to have a go myself—put some of the ideas I had picked up into practice. But it is difficult for a woman. Sometimes I wonder whether I am accepted as a manager. I know I can do the job and am good at it. But there is a funny sort of dividing line between men and women in management. Even though there are many more women in management these days, I don't know what we have achieved by entering management. Many of the old barriers still exist, particularly that acceptance problem. *Woman General Manager, aged 52*

> I have been through it so many times that I know when it is going to occur again. Men just don't want you in the workforce. Your place is in the home and you musn't intrude on their home—the organisation. They will do everything they can to get rid of you— especially if you are a competent woman. You are to be 'seen and not heard', to 'mind your place' and not to 'disturb the status quo'. Of all the women managers I know I don't know of one who is happy or reaching self-actualisation. They just have a grim battle for survival. *Woman Finance Manager, aged 46*

> You have to push your way up, be you a man or a woman. It is a

24-hour a day, seven day a week commitment. You have to watch
what you say, how you will react, how you will respond, and it is
definitely harder for a woman. But maybe it means once again that
the ones that do get there are better than the average male.
Woman Marketing Manager, aged 33

Now that the Decade is over women must take stock. This is a
common practice in retailing—why not in women's careers? Answers
are needed to some serious questions. For instance, are women
achieving by entering management? Are they progressing up the
ladder, or are they being retained in the 'velvet ghettos'—the peripheral staff and service areas of organisations? Are they gaining
the necessary experience for more senior roles, or are they merely
content to do jobs which give them a great sense of self-satisfaction
but not much prestige or status?

You may not be interested in the answers to those questions, being
content to do your 'own thing'. You have a job, a role in society,
friends and family, money to travel and amuse yourself, a suitable partner, and a reputation. These issues don't really concern
you.

On the other hand you may be very interested in the answers. You
may be wondering why, despite all your efforts, you have not yet
made the progress you expected. No matter what you do, how many
extra courses you undertake, the long hours you work—nothing
seems to change. You are blocked, frustrated in your career aims,
with no satisfactory explanation as to the reasons why. The goal
seems to elude you as much as ever. Other women are reaching
senior management—why not you?

Well, don't despair. You are not alone in your need to find the
answers or the elusive path to the top. Despite what you may have
heard to the contrary, women's fight to reach the senior levels has
only just begun. You may have entered the race, but you have been
left behind at the starting blocks. While being given the title of
'manager' may increase your self-esteem, you have to learn to keep
the title and to progress beyond the first hurdles.

TAKING STOCK

The Australian Bureau of Statistics is unable to detail the exact
number of women managers in Australia because their method of
categorisation includes women who are performing functions which
are not strictly managerial. Nevertheless, the official figures indicate

that women in managerial-type positions represent only 16.4 per cent of all employed women workers.

Why is this the case? After all, women have been entering the workforce in greatly increasing numbers since the Second World War. Surely more should have reached management level in that time.

Interestingly, the answer lies in the historical employment situation for women. Throughout this century women have tended to be employed in only a few occupations and industries. Even today the three 'traditional' women's areas—clerical, sales and service, sport and recreation—employ 64 per cent of all women workers. None of these occupations has a reputation for being a training ground for future women managers.

Women have also traditionally been employed in only a few industries, a situation which still applies in the late 1980s. Four main industries—community services; wholesale and retail trade; manufacturing; and finance, property and business services—account for 75 per cent of employed women. Another growth area for women's employment is the entertainment and recreational industry.

The relatively few women managers who exist vis-a-vis their male counterparts have been given their opportunities in the manufacturing and service industries[2]. Another opportunity area is the public sector, where Governments have taken the lead in appointing women to senior positions. However, the mining, primary and heavy industries are not known for their employment opportunities for either women in general or women managers in particular.

So where can women managers be found? In what levels of management are they located and in what functions? Where are the best opportunities for aspiring women? The following figures provide the answers.

A 1984 Survey of Australian business[3] . . .

. . . revealed that only 1706 women held management positions out of a total workforce of 214 820 in 239 major Australian companies. There were also only 45 women in senior management compared to 1873 men. While 11 women were directors, most of these had been appointed since 1980. Reasons given for the paucity of women managers were the conservative nature of Australian business, the traditional dominance of men in certain industries and occupations, and the lack of essential qualifications and experience on the part of the women themselves.

Similar findings were found in a national survey of 62 advertising agencies[4] and in a 1981 survey of major Victorian businesses.[5]

The Australian Public Service . . .

. . . had 1102 women in management (classes 9 to 11) and 88 in the senior executive service in 1986 compared to 81 and 8 respectively in 1975. However, this has only been achieved after considerable effort, a Royal Commission into Australian Government Administration (1975) and the realisation that women were discriminated against by the Public Service Act and its Regulations.[6,7,8] In fact, until 1949 all women in the Australian Public Service, apart from a few professionals, were employed within the Fourth Division—the lowest level. Women were also prevented from having 'careers' by a marriage bar which meant dismissal on marriage (repealed in 1966), 'male only' and 'female only' segregated employment positions (removed in 1973), and an upper age limit which further restricted opportunities for older women. The Australian Public Service is now to the forefront in social change for women's careers, with a woman being appointed Permanent Head of a Department in 1985.

The New South Wales Public Service . . .

. . . has also been improving its opportunities for women managers. These days (1986) over 40 are employed in a senior management capacity compared to two ten years ago. However, like its 'big sister', the Australian Public Service (APS), the NSW Public Service previously put major impediments in the career paths of women—marriage bars and occupational and hierarchical sex-typing being typical hurdles[9]. Women now occupy some very senior positions in the Service, while several have become Permanent Heads of Departments (Pat O'Shane being the first woman and first Aborigine in such a position). However, before you become too euphoric about these achievements, it has taken a very determined Directorate of Equal Employment Opportunity in Public Employment (DEOPE) to effect some of the changes through equal employment and affirmative action programmes. DEOPE has also had the support of the NSW Anti-Discrimination Act.

The Victorian Public Service . . .

. . . like the other two Services, also had a marriage bar, 'male only' and 'female only' positions, and a prohibition on women sitting for the

Administration Examination, which would have admitted them to higher ranks (repealed for women in 1972). A 1983 survey found women to be poorly represented in senior positions[10]. Since then an Agenda for Women has been introduced to help rectify the imbalances. Latest figures to hand (1986) reveal 45 women to be in positions of Class 9 and above.

The Tertiary Education Sector . . .

. . . has had a long tradition of impeding women's progress into senior positions. All tertiary institutions, whether universities, colleges of advanced education, or technical and further education are renowned for their lack of recognition of women employees—particularly the academic professional. Investigations generally reveal that women are concentrated in the lower academic ranks, are more likely to be untenured than male academics, have fewer qualifications than their male colleagues, and receive fewer promotion opportunities.[11,12,13] Poiner (1984)[14] estimated that women represented only 6.8 per cent of appointments at the senior lecturer level and above, with 2.4 per cent of professorial appointments being held by women. However, the new Affirmative Action (Equal Employment Opportunity for Women) Bill (1986) means that the sector will have to remedy this situation because it is the first domain required to take positive steps to improve the employment status of women. Changes should be seen within the next ten years.

The Professions . . .

. . . are also not renowned for high-status opportunities for women. In the area of law, Mathews[15] found that few women received partnerships in law practices. Less than 5 per cent of barristers were women, while women were segregated into conveyancing, estate and family law. The more prestige areas of commercial, company and criminal law were deficient in the number of women practitioners.

Similarly, the Equal Opportunity Board, Victoria,[16] found few women partners in chartered accountancy. Family responsibilities, client resistance, lack of career mindedness in women and the profession's inherent conservatism were cited as the main career impediments to women.

In teaching—a 'woman's' profession—women are also not emerging at the top. 1985 data finds them still at, or close to, the bottom of all education employment hierarchies.[17] While legal barriers have been removed from their career paths, few are applying for promotion.

Where they are, they tend to aspire less highly than men. Their lack of career aspiration is said to be due to a desire to remain in the class-room in contact with students, feeling unable to cope with the extra demands and responsibilities of promotion, and a perceived conflict between after-school commitments and domestic responsibilities.

Social work is another area where women are not following careers in management. Although considered a 'woman's' profession, the senior executive positions in community social service agencies and in tertiary training bodies are typically held by men.[18] Women's discontinuity of employment for childbearing and rearing affects their returning employment prospects (many go part-time), as does their choice of employer (women chose local voluntary agencies as opposed to men, who chose government careers).

Flight-attending is still considered a woman's occupation. By using both negotiation and strike action, women have in recent times removed the no marriage bar, premature retirement, the no glasses rule and the lack of a career path.[19] Until recently, women were also prevented from moving into other areas, for example, becoming airline pilots. In 1979, following a well publicised anti-discrimination case, women were finally allowed to become airline pilots. (While some women are becoming assistant managers of airports, women have not yet made significant moves into airline management.)

Finally, women have been impeded from entering the engineering profession by its overt masculine image and the accompanying perception that it is neither a suitable nor an achievable goal for women, the filtering out of women through prejudicial advice from parents, teachers, school counsellors, careers teachers and guidance officers, and the belief that women themselves either do not want or cannot cope with non-traditional work or leadership positions. As Eileen Byrne concludes: 'No strategies for change will succeed if male attitudes do not learn from the history of women's success over 50 years in the profession, and accept them as equal partners and professional colleagues in the economic development of our country.'[20] As with the majority of professions, engineering has a long way to go before women are given opportunities and gain acceptance as management material.

Does this summary surprise you? It shouldn't, because this is the reality today for women in many parts of management. Each of the employment sectors examined reveals that women managers occupy mainly junior positions in organisations with only a few reaching senior positions. Women are also segregated into specialist and peripheral roles in management and are generally treated as outsiders in a traditionally male-dominated environment. Management is still a largely male enclave.

KEEPING THE STATUS QUO

With such dismal news you may be wondering whether it is worth the effort to keep on trying. Of course it is. The above information was necessary to remind you that things take time to change. Women tend to forget that major impediments prevented their pursuit of almost any career until fairly recent times. Moreover, it has taken major social change, such as new legislation in the form of equal employment opportunity and affirmative action, to effect even the smallest improvements in the status of women. Most of this has been overlooked lately as the media extol the virtues of the 'new' successful woman. Patience is required, as well as an understanding of how the many and varied forces have operated to keep you 'in your place'.

Apart from the more structural impediments such as 'no marriage' bars, there are some other covert strategies which have successfully prevented women from reaching their full employment potential. These strategies are not even realised or tend to be overlooked in the quest for the 'numbers game'. Taken together, however, they have a devastating impact on the status of women, though you may have been completely unaware of them. These covert strategies are discussed below.

Divide and Conquer

If you have often wondered why you have not had the same opportunities or wages as men it is because there has been a 'divide and conquer' rule operating in the job market place. Unbeknown to you, you have been looking for jobs within the 'secondary labour market'. This is the term given to a job market which has low wages, poor working conditions, few opportunities for advancement and little job security.[21,22,23] Most of the job seekers in this market are women. In fact, the opportunity to compete for and be allocated to this labour market rests mainly on *ascribed* characteristics of race and gender.

You may have been unaware of this market because it is not acknowledged that it exists. However, labour law practice helped create the market originally when women were officially granted 'secondary' status with lower wage rates by the Arbitration Commission. While equal pay is supposed to be a reality these days, it is not a fact of life in many areas. Hence women are kept in this market because of past practices and tradition.

Alternatively, men occupy the 'primary labour market' because labour law has historically enshrined them as society's 'breadwinners'. They thus receive better employment positions and higher pay than women.

This dual labour market also operates within management. Recent surveys have shown that women are not receiving the more senior, responsible or well paid positions in this arena either.[24,25] The dual labour market, a term introduced by labour economists and not feminists, has obstructed women's entry to certain occupations and industries and ultimately their entry and acceptance in mangement.

Consider the case of Marilyn, aged 38, who is still attempting to find her right place in management:

> I don't know what there is about me, but I just don't seem to be able to win. Every time I go for a job I never get the same pay as my male colleagues, and when I leave they usually appoint two people to fill my place—a male and a female—and give the male a fancy title and lots more money.
>
> This happened in my last company. I was in charge of a department and had about seven women working for me. I had been there five years and thought I was being reasonably well treated. Then I began to check around some of my women friends who worked for other companies and found that my salary was about $10 000 below theirs. I seemed to have a much more senior job and a lot more responsibility. I went to see the Personnel Manager; who was quite surprised when I asked him for a review of my salary. He said: 'Oh! you were reviewed some time ago. We didn't do anything about you because you have never complained and you seemed to be happy. You'll now have to wait until the next review. I don't know when that will take place because the firm is having to cut back'.
>
> I was so annoyed at both the treatment and my own passive attitude that I approached a management consultant I knew and got myself 'head hunted'. Apparently doing a good job was not sufficient to earn a salary rise—you had to go and complain! I'm now earning about what I think I should, but I can't be sure. There is this terrible secrecy about salaries. The senior management likes to camouflage it by talking about 'packages'—you know, your package is different to mine and so they just can't be equated.
>
> What really got to me in my last company was that they had to appoint two people to replace me. A woman who did all the work I was doing, and a man who was brought in at a higher level, given a very fancy title and lots of perks (otherwise he would not take the job), and $20 000 difference in salary (to go with the title).

That's how they beat you in the end—give the fellows a fancy title to justify the salary. He knows nothing about the work, and the woman will do it all for him. However, he will get the credit and the career. I didn't even get a thank-you when I left. In fact, management seemed to be peeved that I had left them in the 'lurch' and they had to spend more money to replace me.

Keeping us in our stations—Part 1

Another successful strategy to block your attempts at progress is to claim that you have certain employment 'deficiencies' because of your female upbringing. Because women have traditionally and culturally occupied the more passive and nurturing roles in society, the skills learnt in these arenas are thought to be unsuitable for the workplace. Consequently, employers and the community alike assume that women lack the necessary skills, abilities and requisites to function effectively in certain jobs and industries. Classic examples are the past practices of refusing women entry to 'heavy industry', apprenticeships in trades, and the engineering profession.

Women's role socialisation, and perceived lack of aggression, also acts as a barrier in management. Women are not seen to 'fit' the managerial model for success and are retained in the lower echelons of organisational life. The pressure is on women to be 'feminine' and to avoid competing in a 'man's' world, especially in the power and decision-making areas.

If you have been brought up to be 'feminine', then you face some difficult hurdles. You were probably told that conformity to this norm would bring you the accolade of being 'a good girl'. However, the workplace will penalise you for this because you will be considered to be insufficiently aggressive or dominant, unable to make 'difficult and hard' decisions. Should you attempt to rectify this by acting more assertively you will then be considered to be 'unfeminine', 'a dragon', and 'a bad manager'. Like it or not, your role socialisation makes it very difficult for you to win respect in both the workplace and management.

Adelle reports a current case in her organisation:

We had a woman appointed from outside into senior management a little while ago. In fact, she is running one of our major divisions—a very difficult job. She has had senior management positions before and came with a good reputation. Everyone was pleased to welcome her and word soon spread that she was a 'lady'. She speaks well, dresses beautifully and is very considerate of everyone. She is also a listener which is pretty rare around here.

However, the union took one look at her and pronounced her a 'pushover'. Everything went well for a few months and then the union began to get active—over silly little things. She soon found that her time was being taken up with trivial complaints, all of which were blown up out of all proportion by the union. I've noticed lately that management is also getting restive. Word is going around that she doesn't have it in her to make the 'hard' decisions, that she's too soft, that what we want around here is a MAN to run that division. I don't know how true these stories are, but it seems that her approach is at fault. She is just too feminine and everyone is now beginning to take advantage of her or taking no notice of her at all. It's a great shame because she offers a different style of management and could have been a role model for all the other women in the organisation.

Keeping us in our stations—Part 2

Organisations have another method of keeping you out of management and especially the more senior levels. Based once more on tradition and past practice, an 'internal' labour market or 'sex structured' hierarchy can successfully thwart your aspirations if you are an ambitious woman. This strategy, either deliberate or otherwise, works as follows. First, jobs are differentiated within the organisation into male and female jobs. These jobs are then ordered hierarchically so that males are more senior than females and are not expected to take orders from females. Power is enshrined in the male gender. The result is a gender power differential which operates within the organisation in addition to basic gender differences and the gender segregation of the workforce.

Wendy, aged 31, and attempting to build a career in a bank, describes how this strategy can work:

The Personnel Manager called me in and offered me a job in the Customer Service area. He told me that the bank was opening up a whole new Division to give women a chance. I was to be the Manager in charge, and would have a team of women working for me. The Personnel Manager told me that the 'powers above' were very excited by this proposal because the bank would become recognised as a leader in developing women's careers. He went on to explain the structure and how everything would work. He summed up by saying that women could now have a career in an area in which they were good—customer service and dealing with people.

I was horrified. Here was this organisation in which I was struggling to make a career, siphoning me off into a woman's ghetto and ensuring that I would never get to the top. When I asked him how I would make the transition back into the areas that mattered—like foreign exchange—he seemed perplexed. He said I didn't have to—I had a career where I was—in good old customer service. There would be two parallel hierarchies—one for men, and one for women. The bank was certainly giving us a *great chance*! What they were really doing was ensuring that the men got all the top jobs—those with any authority—and we were to be content with a service area.

This form of social ordering in organisations ensures that women are recruited into positions of passivity and compliance and men into positions of dominance and authority. The practice helps explain two aspects of women's employment: why they are found in certain organisational roles and not in others; and why there are so few in senior positions, even though there may be many in the lower management levels. It also explains why some women have difficulty in establishing a career within the one organisation. Because they are unable to progress up the hierarchical ladder, they have to move around organisations in order to get promotion. However, they may still be thwarted in their career goals if the organisations they move to also adopt this strategy.

Men rule the world

Feminists and sociologists believe that most work organisations are dominated by a patriarchal philosophy. Patriarchy is a fashionable term these days to explain women's 'oppression' in the workforce. Briefly, it means 'a complex set of social relations, within and by which, men tend to dominate women'.[26] Similar to the strategy discussed above, it 'accords higher value to the activities, and greater power to the person, of those assigned to the male rather than the female gender'[27].

Sociologists have established that a patriarchal orientation governs most professions. Patriarchy is also said to be increasingly evident in the semi-professions of nursing, social work and teaching.[28,29] As they become more like full professions men are becoming more dominant because of their differential promotion over women as managers rather than practitioners. Men apply for the management roles, while the women are content to remain as 'operators'. The profession thus naturally becomes male-led, leading to the transposition of a male management philosophy and its various consequences.

Women on the fringe

A final strategy often used by organisations against 'invading hordes' is to keep them on the 'margin' and away from the 'centre' of power and decision-making. This is kept safely in a few trusted hands. 'Fringe dwellers' are never offered the keys to the 'inner sanctum' because that would remove them from their peripheral roles.

Most 'fringe dwellers' in organisations are women—although occasionally ethnic workers also come into that category. Marginal people are primarily those whom the organisation does not want to accept. The lack of acceptance can be for many reasons, but essentially it is based on the fact that the aspirant does not 'fit in'.

The concept of marginality explains a great deal about the current status of women managers. For instance, it helps explain their uncertain and unpredictable acceptance in organisations, their appointment to peripheral roles, not mainstream or line management, the obstacles preventing them from becoming fully integrated into their management groups or organisations, and the negative stereotyping, prejudicial attacks and discriminatory treatment they so often receive. It is thus not so much of a strategy as a process underlying women managers' current status. Women are so busy attempting to build their careers that they don't realise that they have only been granted the status of 'fringe dwellers' in organisations. If they wish to succeed they will have to leave these peripheral areas and move into the 'mainstream' of organisational life.

HOW TO WIN THROUGH

By now you may be feeling that you will never be able to overcome these strategies and hurdles which so effectively limit your career. It just doesn't seem fair after all your commitment, sacrifice and dedication. You feel so *alone*. There must be an easier way to earn a living and to reach senior management. You will just wait until the Government introduces social changes that advantage you, or retire to a less stressful life.

That's your decision and you are free to make it. But remember that virtually every woman who has achieved high managerial status has had to go through this same grind. She has faced the situations, analysed her options and moved accordingly. What makes her so different to you is that she has become 'street smart'! She has seen what was needed to be done, and responded. She has become positive about her career, rather than letting it all 'happen' to her. She has

adopted a strategy, one that has allowed her to survive and *win*.
† What is this strategy that makes her more successful than you? Be
prepared for some hard decisions and a change in attitude. For
instance:

- You will just have to decide whether or not you are really serious
  about a career. Successful people do not 'give it a try for a few
  years' and then opt out when circumstances become difficult.
  They just keep on going despite all the handicaps, hurdles and
  obstacles. Unfortunately, too many women fantasise about having
  a career. They want a home, marriage, children, an exciting job,
  fame, glamour and riches. What they are not prepared for are the
  sacrifices that this entails. No woman has ever reached senior
  management without having made some significant sacrifices
  along the way. The sacrifice may entail marriage, children,
  health, peace of mind. However, a choice has to be made
  because the career demands single-mindedness. Avoid the all-
  consuming dedication and the goals are not achieved.
  Decision rule no. 1: Decide whether or not you *want* a career.
  Once having made the decision, *keep going and don't look back.*

- Our successful woman then decides where this career can be
  best established. Instead of wandering around organisations or
  consultants looking for a job in order to 'get my start', she has a
  particular industry or occupation in mind. She will approach
  various organisations and offer her services. If she is
  sophisticated, she will even indulge in marketing ploys to gain
  attention. Sometimes she may be given the job she seeks. Quite
  often she is asked to serve an 'apprenticeship' at a much lower
  level which, if she is sensible, she will take. The idea is to gain
  credibility by earning the 'brownie points' in accordance with that
  organisation's value system.

- Having gained entry to an organisation, she begins to research
  what constitutes success in that industry or occupation. Is it
  marketing, finance, sales, production or personnel? Is it policy
  areas, research areas, operational areas? Is it a generalist role or
  a specialist role? Whatever it is, she then begins to align her
  career goals with what will be the shortest route to high
  managerial status. She does not get diverted along the way by
  'interesting jobs', 'dead-end jobs', or 'women's career jobs'. She
  knows that the shortest distance between point A and point B is a
  straight line.
  Decision rule no. 2: *no deviations from the career path.*

- Our successful woman also knows that every career has a time frame. You must be in certain positions by a certain age or you are considered to be 'past your prime' and 'inflexible to change'. Again, you could be marked as 'not having quite made it'. You must be at a certain hierarchical level by the time you are in your early forties or you will never be appointed to senior management (unless you own the company!). So you should aim to spend only a certain number of years in each position en route to a senior position. It gets much harder to move quickly as you move up the hierarchy. Hence, most movement should take place early in the career.
  Decision rule no. 3: *keep a watch on the time frame.*

- She knows that office politics, economic circumstances, mergers and takeovers may thwart her straight line to the top. In other words, the career may proceed according to plan for a while and then suddenly run into ambushes and obstacles. Careful analysis reveals that these are not going to go away. Indeed, they are being carefully staged to ensure that our woman manager can *proceed no further.* So she does not waste time. *She leaves the organisation for another and a step up the ladder.*
  Decision rule no. 4: *if careers are thwarted find another organisation which will allow further room to move.*

- She also avoids 'women's' work ghettos. She knows that to succeed she has to be able to mix with both genders. While work in a 'woman's' area can be very satisfying, it is not the type of work which usually runs the organisation, unless it is a woman's refuge.
  Decision rule no. 5: *avoid women's enclaves—find out where the men work and go there.*

- The successful woman manager also avoids specialist roles which have no real managerial responsibility and goes straight for line management. She is not content to have a job with managerial status but no power and authority. She wants to be *boss.* This means that she must *manage* people and budgets—perhaps even make *money.* No one has ever reached top management without serving apprenticeships in line management.
  Decision rule no. 6: *forget about the 'nice' jobs—learn how to be a boss in continually expanding departments!*

- The successful woman manager also is not averse to helping her own career. If she finds that the organisation does not have the job she wants, she will create a *need.* That is, she will present rational and reasoned arguments for the creation of a new job, division or department—all in the interests of the organisation. As she is usually the one with the most knowledge about this new area, she is likely to be appointed to start it off.

Decision rule no. 7: *create your own opportunities.*

■ Finally, she may find that despite her careful planning she is not achieving her goal. She has the experience, the qualifications, the dedication and commitment, but is continually passed over in favour of less competent men. Does she give up? No. She does her homework (researches the feasibility), pulls in her favours, uses her 'contacts' and opens her own business (quite often taking a sizeable slice of her former organisation's business with her). It may be a small organisation, but she is the boss, the organisation bears her name, and she has the capacity and experience to succeed. So,

Decision rule no. 8: *when all else fails, try your wings and become an entrepreneur!*

THE CHOICE

You may feel that this type of strategy is not for you. It looks too much like scheming, and you just don't operate that way. Also the successful woman manager seems to be quite ruthless about her career ambitions. If anything gets in her way she finds a way around it. This is not you. You don't believe in such tactics. You would prefer to retain your friends and your reputation of being a 'nice' person. You don't want to be called 'ruthless', 'dangerous', and 'ambitious'. You just want to be accepted and to be allowed to do your job your way.

Well, if you do think like this you are merely fantasising about a career and your wish for success. Successful people usually stage-manage their careers as outlined above. Interview any successful man or woman and similar themes emerge. Different terminology may occasionally be used, but the steps are there. It is a well tried and trusted route to top management. It is there for others to follow providing they have the necessary commitment and dedication.

If you can accept this, then success can be yours. All you may have to do is to re-orient yourself occasionally to the straight and narrow path. You may also have to acquire some courage to try some of the strategies. After all, it can sometimes be quite harrowing working in an all-male group, and line management can be very stressful. There will be times when it will *not* seem worthwhile! Why should you be the one who is harassed, who is so tired at the end of the day from meetings and decisions, and who feels that the compensations are not sufficient for the time, energy and effort required? Such black moments are a twilight time for every manager. However, most successful people are managers, unless they happen to be employed in specialist professional roles. Yet even here management skills are needed to maintain offices and to supply the specialist services.

3

How women are kept at bay

WHAT YOU ARE UP AGAINST

Congratulations! You have taken the advice, made your career choice, and decided to aim for top management. You are prepared to face the hurdles and all you want is the chance to put your persuasive ideas into practice. Hard work and determination will do the rest.

Well, what we have not prepared you for is the fact that women are *not* generally accepted in management. Oh! That's not true, you say. What about the media reports of women 'superstars'? Surely these women are accepted or they would not have risen to such heights? Why say these things when you are trying to encourage women to consider top management? It will just put them off.

The fact is if you wish to succeed it is important that you know about the barriers that lie ahead. With knowledge comes power and a chance to overcome some of the hurdles. For too long women have been kept in the dark in order that the 'divide and conquer' rule could apply. Management is one of the last bastions for women to access. No-one said it was going to be easy. Each step has to be *earned*. Success has to be *merited*. You should try to recognise the barriers for what they are, rather than take them personally, if you are to take defensive action.

One of the first things you will encounter are the unflattering comments people make about women in management. These comments may not be made to you, or about you, although this is always possible in these days of participatory management. Usually they are expressed about other women friends or colleagues, or just women in general. When first encountered they can be a little hard to bear, as there is always that niggling feeling that you are included in the generalisation. In time, however, you learn to counter the comments through either performance, familiarity or just plain common sense.

Consider these opinions, which emerged during the *Women in Management Study* referred to in the foreword.

> I don't believe women should be in management. They only get hard and lose their femininity. You just can't talk to them either—they're either moody, jealous, temperamental, picky or they want to control everything. Give me a man any day—at least you know where you are with them. *Woman non-manager, aged 42*

> You just couldn't have a woman as managing director of BHP. I mean, she just wouldn't know what to do. Who would listen to her? The shareholders, the financial press, the Japanese? You must have a man if you want credibility. *Male manager, aged 56*

> If you let a woman run anything important it would soon be in a mess. A woman's place is in the home. That's her biological function and you just can't get away from that fact of life. Women have no head for figures—imagine them trying to balance the country's budget. They're just not used to thinking in big terms as you must in business. *Male non-manager, aged 38*

Other studies confirm that these are not atypical opinions.[1,2,3] These attitudes still exist despite changing social times. The right of women to work has not been accompanied by a right to hold authority and power. Although they may often be the breadwinners or hold higher positions and earn more than their husbands, women are still considered to occupy a less important role in the economic fabric.[4] Consequently, when their abilities and talents are judged within the occupational arena women are evaluated in terms of whether or not they have 'failed as a woman' rather than whether they have been successful in a career or a management position.

WHY AREN'T YOU ACCEPTED?

Women tend not to be accepted in management because their very presence is surrounded by myths and stereotypes. These arise for two reasons: women have traditionally played a nurturing and mothering role in society, and they are now leaving this to enter the male managerial world.

Most Australian organisations, both public and private, adopt a particular model of managerial behaviour. Briefly, this model depicts managers as being rational, efficient and unemotional when performing their daily tasks. These particular qualities are usually associated with men rather than women. In contrast, the stereotypical view of women is that they are emotional, irrational, dependent, unable to make decisions[5] and are therefore not suited to management.

Interestingly, this preference for masculine-type traits arose because few female managers existed, if at all, when the profile of the 'ideal' manager was established. Consequently, when most people think 'manager' they usually think 'male'. Managers and employees are so used to this version of the 'ideal' manager that few feel any need to change their expectations or beliefs. The masculine model is accepted as normal and women are the ones who are expected to 'fit in'.

Douglas McGregor, the well known organisational theorist, explains the situation more fully:

> The model of a successful manager in our culture is a masculine one. The good manager is aggressive, competitive, firm, just. He is not feminine; he is not soft and yielding or dependent or intuitive in the womanly sense. The very expression of emotion is widely viewed as a feminine weakness that would interfere with effective business practices.[6]

As a manager, or an aspiring one, you will just have to accept that you are entering a masculine world. In fact many women find that in order to succeed in management they have to model their behaviour on the examples set by male managers. So powerful are the beliefs and attitudes that women are 'outsiders' to this culture, that younger women managers have been found to accept strongly the masculine model[7] while female MBA students have fitted the masculine managerial image more closely than their male counterparts.[8] The phrase 'she is just one of us' is your accolade for conforming to the male managerial model.

MYTHS AND STEREOTYPES

Given that women are not accepted in management, how does the system operate against you? The following list includes a number of stereotypical excuses which have at one time or other been used successfully to exclude women from management:

1 Women are more emotional and sensitive to the feelings of others, while men are rational and coolly objective in their relationships with others.
2 Women are uncomfortable in a man's world.
3 Women work as a hobby or for luxuries and, as a result, lack the ambition, aggressiveness and dedication necessary to excel in business.
4 Women have higher rates of sickness and absenteeism.
5 Women do not understand statistics.[9]
6 Women are too 'emotional' for business.
7 Working women threaten the authority of the males in the workplace and at home.
8 Women who successfully venture into the world of business often pay for it by an erosion of their femininity.[10]
9 Men are intellectually superior.
10 Men value achievements, promotion and meaningful work more than women.
11 Men are inherently more assertive than women.
12 The successful manager must possess masculine attributes.[11]

It may sound extreme, but these attitudes are rarely challenged in the workplace. The following comments appeared in a 1986 issue of *The Financial Australian*:

All the signs sent to top management from middle female management suggest that the young female executive on the way up wants all the privileges of management, while retaining all the traditional cop-outs . . .

These cop-outs have, in the past, been the unspoken compensations for the less important positions women occupied in the workplace.

Female middle-management executives, it is contended, have more days away sick.

They tend, more often than males, to be late for meetings and appointments, take longer lunch hours and want to get away before the traffic gets too heavy.

Of course this is a generalisation. There are many exceptions, but as a general comment it seems female executives try to modify the working environment to suit themselves.[12]

Although ample evidence exists to suggest that not all women 'fit' these stereotypes (just think of the women you know and how removed from reality these comments are), it seems that these images will persist until more women are in management. So be prepared to see them emerge occasionally either in the media, as in the case above, or in surveys which attempt to elicit attitudes towards women in management (as in the *Women in Management Study*).

EFFECTS OF THE MYTHS AND STEREOTYPES

To take defensive action against these myths and stereotypes the first thing you will have to forget is your *uniqueness*! Despite what you may think about yourself, the myths and stereotypes will not let your particular individuality shine through. This is because *all* women are judged to be the *same*. This makes it easier for others to relate to you, because they assume that all women have the same characteristics, instead of being individuals. Any uniqueness (like being brilliant at planning and coordinating) is simply overlooked because it does not fit into the stereotypical view of women. If you are regarded in this fashion your long-term career may be affected by erroneous and spurious judgements made by an unthinking individual.

Also, the gender bias inherent in the stereotypes may result in your being compared unfavourably to men on some attribute or performance criterion. For instance, women are not thought to be as aggressive or as competitive as men. Should an employment interviewer think this way, you may not be appointed to certain positions, like line management. Being extremely capable, trustworthy and having a 'track record' is not enough to overcome this stereotypical hurdle! The interviewer simply believes you can't do the task because of particular 'deficiencies'. This type of gender bias has other consequences. You may receive a lower starting salary and face closed access to higher level jobs.[13] Although legislation now exists to prohibit these forms of discrimination, studies suggest that a number still apply within management.[14,15]

Should you overcome this hurdle and be appointed to management, the stereotypes can still affect you. You may receive slower rates of promotion, assignment to less attractive or challenging tasks, lower and/or less frequent salary rises, fewer training opportunities and placement in dead-end positions—that is, jobs with no career 'potential'.[16] In fact, certain occupations and roles in organisations and industries have become 'sex-typed' as a result of these forms of discrimination. Although legislation now exists to prohibit them, the evidence on industrial and occupational segregation suggests that it will be some time before these consequences are remedied.

Interestingly, many women accept the stereotypes and believe that they *are* incapable of managing. They thus conform to the 'self-fulfilling prophecy'. Others are afraid of losing their 'femininity'—however that is defined. If you maintain these attitudes then you are voluntarily diminishing your own career aspirations.

Some women are content to accept their societal role because derogatory labels are applied to those who break the stereotypes, such as 'the queen bee', 'the iron maiden', 'the dragon', 'the bitch', or, more simply, 'I wouldn't like to be like *her*'. They discriminate against themselves by refusing to enter either the workplace or certain roles or occupations. Their acceptance of the stereotypes effectively limits their progress.

ARE THE MYTHS REAL?

Generally no, but people tend to approximate them with reality because they have never been encouraged to question them. Women managers are thus perceived in certain ways, irrespective of what they do.

Luckily, evidence now exists to refute many of the stereotypes. For instance, overseas research has established that women are similar to men in leadership style and behaviour, in potential managerial capability, in cooperation and competition, in problem solving and in sources of job satisfaction and motivation. Subordinates have also been found to achieve as much satisfaction under a woman boss as under a male boss.

Again, an exhaustive American study of nearly 2000 managers,[17] revealed only two differences in managerial behaviour between male and female managers. The first favoured females: they were more 'achieving' in their work motivation profiles than their male counterparts. The second favoured male managers: they were more interpersonally competent with their colleagues than were females. However, the general conclusion was that women were no different from men in their performance of the management function.

Despite this encouraging news, you may find that as a manager you are still judged in terms of stereotypes. In fact, the stereotypes have remained remarkably stable over the past decade despite general changes in social attitudes.[18,19] Moreover, men have been the most consistently negative in their attitudes towards women managers.[20] Until these attitudes can be overcome, then, you should not be too elated by the evidence that you can manage as effectively as a man!

THE AUSTRALIAN SCENE

How do Australians react to women managers? Are we as progressive in encouraging competent women as we were with early votes for women and child endowment? Or are we also trapped in the gender role morass which ensures that women achievers are considered abnormal?

Australians seem to have difficulty understanding those women who want more than a home and marriage. This attitude is summarised by the following comment from the *Women in Management Study*:

> Being happily married with four children I have no desire to go out to work. However, I was very good at maths at school and was a computer programmer before I was married and I can understand women who want to pursue a career. Nevertheless, I feel children, as a whole, miss out if their mother works (both parents) as nothing can replace being home to greet the children when they come home from school or when they need you. Their needs cannot be met in the hour or so given to them each night by a working mother. I manage to fill in a full day as it is and I know that if I worked my husband and children would be the losers. *Woman non-manager, aged 38*

This pervasive view sums up how many Australians (women as well as men) feel about women in management, although in fact, the study found that women were the ones particularly in favour of women managers. Among the findings of this survey of 1093 managers, future managers and non-managers were these:

■ The 500 women held significantly more positive attitudes towards women in management than the 593 men (positive attitudes meaning they scored higher on most, if not all, attitudinal items in a questionnaire at a statistically significant level)

■ Some 590 people (who were mainly women) had actually worked for a woman and were supportive of their role in management. The remainder, who had not, were mainly men, and held some fairly traditional views, such as 'pregnancy makes women less desirable than men as employees' (item in questionnaire), and 'women who stay at home all the time with children are better mothers than those who work part-time'. They also felt that women allowed their emotions to influence their managerial behaviour, that they did better in sub-managerial positions, and that they did not want to hold managerial positions (all items in questionnaire).

■ The most supportive group as regards women in management were the 198 women managers, followed closely by the 158 female future managers (business students). The least supportive were the 257 male future managers (business students) and the 101 male non-managers.

These findings mirror the overseas studies, which have also shown that women are the most supportive of women managers[21,22,23] while male students are the most conservative in attitude towards them.[24,25] So it would seem that stereotypical views about women in management are universal. Australia is no different; in fact it has failed to live up to its earlier promise of being a leader in radical social change and instead has tended to follow overseas thinking and to preserve traditional gender roles.

WILL WOMEN MANAGERS EVER BE ACCEPTED?

There is no easy answer to this question. There is, at best, ambivalence:

> I am not sure of my own feelings on the subject of women in management and swing in attitude frequently. I am a 39 year old male and have had bad experiences with female superiors in laboratory-work situations. This has left me feeling biased against women bosses. Yet I think, logically, women have as much right as men to positions of management. *Male non-manager, 39*

> I find no reason to differentiate between male and female management. I do not have a sex-based view towards them. I have run the ambit from befuddled incompetence to scintillating brilliance. Anyone who could question the efficiency of a Buttrose, Thatcher or Gandhi would be a fool. I do feel, however, that we have now reached a stage of giving managerial positions to women as a sinecure to silence the strident, braying feminist

lobby; even having reached the point of reverse sexism. I believe that a stage is being reached when a reaction amongst male managerial staff will set in and a strong anti-women-in-management movement will result. I find sexism to have become a socially divisive issue. *Male manager, aged 40*

In case you think the latter is an isolated opinion, a 1986 issue of *The Bulletin*[26] suggests that an anti-women-in-anything (and not just management) movement has already started. Arguing against attempts to change the promotion criteria for women in academia, Dr Geoffrey Partington commented:

Another example is the assertion that any failure by universities to provide first-class, free child-minding facilities on campus is unfairly discriminatory. A generation ago feminists indignantly denied that the employment of women, including married women with children, would increase costs; now feminists proudly draw attention to the extra costs involved and demand that requisite funding be provided forthwith.

The same change has taken place in relationship to arguments about the effects of pre-menstrual tension, pregnancy and other gynaecological conditions: earlier feminists claimed that these made little or no difference to women's work, now it is claimed that these effects are so considerable that full allowance for them should be built into the structure of employment . . .

. . . however . . . no convincing evidence . . . is ever offered [sic] that even one woman has been denied a seniority appointment or promotion in favor of a less qualified man.

Before you become defensive over this comment, the following reply, written by another male academic, appeared in the next issue of *The Bulletin*:

Poor Geoffrey Partington, how I feel for you, having to share your academic perch with women. They really are such trying creatures, you know. We have a couple in our department, too, so you'll know what I mean when I say they really do mess up the status quo. More verbally skilled at an earlier age, longer living, wholistic learners, emotionally tuned into life and people and now (horrors!) politically inclined and getting a share of the research grants cake. I think you've got the right idea, old man. Let's ban them from the 3Rs, starting next year. Teach them to play in our sand pit, eh what? *M.R. McCully, South Perth.*[27]

However, other commentators think like Dr Partington, as evidenced by this report from Bryce Courtenay in a September 1986 issue of *The Financial Australian*:

> Men are, I fear, beginning to feel a little crowded by the women's movement.
>
> After all, we are not individually very well equipped to fight a determined movement or, for that matter, a determined woman.
>
> Perhaps the women's movement might given us a few pointers on how the two sexes should behave with each other in the workplace?...
>
> The corporate male is genuinely feeling threatened and doesn't quite know what to do—which almost certainly means he will begin to gang up.[28]

Ambitious women need to keep a watchful eye out for developments such as these. It could herald the return of the 'dark ages' when opportunities for women were very limited. Although at the moment statements such as the ones above are still relatively few, it may pay you to start collecting some effective and perhaps non-feminist oriented arguments.

Most people are aware that women are not generally accepted in management. The 1093 Australians in the *Women in Management Study* felt that women managers were accepted by less than 50 per cent of men in business and the community in general. So much for progress and equal rights for women! You will just have to accept that the cultural milieu does not allow for women having the right to hold positions of authority. While claims are made that the situation is altering (due to equal opportunity and affirmative action), the above results tend to suggest that it is static.

Given these considerations, how do the general attitudes affect the employment opportunities of men and women to management positions? For instance, who would Australians employ in a management position given a male and female candidate of *equal* standing (if such equality is possible)? Like it or not, the overwhelming answer from 1093 Australians is the *male*. Why? Because:

> The male would be better accepted by co-workers and subordinates. *Male manager, 25*
>
> Being a male, I would most likely choose a male. *Male manager, 33*
>
> I believe men stay in a job longer and even in the 1980s they are more committed to a career. *Male manager, 34*
>
> Men don't go through emotional stages the same way that women do. *Male future manager, 21*
>
> Dependability—a man will not leave when married, get pregnant and become irrational. *Male future manager, 21*

A man in case of emergencies and disasters. *Male non-manager, 65*

A man because he has to support a family or some day will. *Woman non-manager, 21*

Society still dictates that man is the breadwinner. *Woman future manager, 20*

Who would Australians employ if the female candidate had *superior* qualifications and experience to the male? Overwhelmingly, the *female.* Why? Because:

- Women should be given more opportunity

- The job should go to the applicant with the best qualifications and experience

The real significance of these apparently supportive statements is that they are only made when women have obviously *superior* qualifications. Some die-hards still prefer men, no matter how capable the woman. For example:

I don't like the idea of women in management positions. *Woman future manager, 24*

A married woman with children should stay at home. *Woman non-manager, 55* [This was a common response from many older women.]

So much for women supporting other women! It is not only men who resent ambitious women; it is also women who do not share their ambitions. Apparently women are supposed to abide by the old saying: 'God bless the Squire and his relations and keep us in our proper stations'. Women wanting to be a success in management are just breaking the rules!

ROLE 'TRAPS' FOR WOMEN

How can you escape the stereotypes and negative attitudes? Unfortunately, only with great difficulty. In fact you may be forced to go ahead, and just do your job, while carrying the stereotypes around with you like a snail's shell. You may have to play an 'undesirable' role in your organisation; you may be subject to, and suffer the consequences of, labelling; and your day-to-day effectiveness may be eroded by lack of acceptance and subsequent non-credibility.

Rosabeth Kanter[29] says that women, because of male dominance and the subsequent 'token' position of women, tend to play either the role of 'mother', 'seductress', 'pet' or 'iron maiden' in work organisations. These roles enable your male counterparts to both respond to and understand your presence in situations such as management. Should you fall into one of these role traps you will be forced to live up to the 'image' even though your values, ideas and code of behaviour may be to the contrary. The role enables your male counterparts to handle your sexuality, and their reactions to it, in the workplace.

What does the mother role do to you? Because you are perceived as a 'nurturer', you will be expected to look after your colleagues and do little things for them, be non-critical of their activities, non-threatening in terms of competition for top jobs and provide emotional support when they feel 'down and out'. While you may enjoy this role, it will prevent you from establishing your own identity as a successful manager and from being rewarded for your own achievements.

The seductress role highlights your 'femininity' or 'sexuality'. While appealing if you are a 'feminine' woman, you will be viewed as a sex object, that is, sexually desirable and potentially available. Your male colleagues will respond with alacrity. Some will want to be your 'protector'; others will want to form alliances; others will be resentful if you ignore them; while most will become very annoyed if you direct all your attentions to the boss. You will certainly gain attention in this role. However, your job performance will go unnoticed. While you may feel that you are recognised as a 'woman', this role trap is hardly a good qualification for senior management!

The pet role places you in an adolescent time-lock. You will be expected to be the cheer leader who sits on the sidelines and admires the prowess of your male colleagues. No matter what you do, you will be perceived as 'too young', 'doesn't have any experience', 'not mature enough yet', and 'she's just like my younger sister'. It will be almost impossible for you to demonstrate any skill or competence because you will be expected to admire others—not emulate or outshine them. You will also have to be self-effacing to be accepted in this role.

Finally, the iron maiden role is the least flattering role for women. While it indicates strength of purpose and determination, you are viewed with suspicion by your colleagues, treated with undue and exaggerated politeness and kept at a distance. You may also be labelled 'tough and dangerous'. Most women in this role trap have unwittingly lived up to expectations by adopting militant behaviour. However, Mrs Thatcher is often called the 'iron maiden' by foreign countries and this label does not seem to have done her any harm. In fact it seems to have improved her success around the negotiating table! A bonus point for reaching senior management?

These distorted views appear to have arisen because of the lack of women in management. Kathryn Bartol[30] says that 'tokens' are also perceived as less serious in intentions than a man, are forced into non-relevant and non-productive roles, acquire deviant labels of non-conformity, and face possible expulsion or 'voluntary' withdrawal from a group because of lack of acceptance.

In case you think there are no token women in Australian organisations, examine the following comment from a 35-year-old woman manager in the publishing business:

> I am the senior woman in the company and have a staff of just on ten people. However, I find that I am not accepted by my male peers even though in many cases I have much more responsibility than they do. When it comes to power and decision-making I find that I am usually left out. I may have attended a meeting and thought that something was decided. But then I find that the men have re-grouped at a later meeting and another decision has been made. I am not consulted at all—not even informed—yet it usually affects my area. I don't know how you overcome this problem. I have thought about it a lot because I want to progress in the company. I think I am treated as a junior colleague even though I have senior rank. Some of the men have made comments like: 'Well, it's about time you grew up and got blood on your hands', and 'You have to learn to be tough'. Recently I have tried being persistent in meetings and it has caused some reactions—normally I have tried to treat people pleasantly and courteously but have just been overridden. So I am now sticking to my point and refusing to give in. My colleagues don't know how to handle this. I feel this is the only way to go if I am to be treated seriously.

Jane, aged 45 and a senior manager and associate director of a large market research company, states her situation:

> I have noticed that when I go to board meetings the men don't know how to react to me. Sometimes some of the senior women are invited to a meeting and it becomes just like an old-fashioned dance in the country. The men on one side having their little 'huddle' and deciding what to do and the women on the other waiting to be asked to join in. The men just don't know how to communicate—I think that's the problem. They are so used to us being at lower levels in the organisation that they just don't know what to say. So a couple of the women and I have got together and

we have decided that it is up to us to break this down. Otherwise
we will never get a chance. We will have to teach the senior men
how to relate to us instead of being threatened by us.

These are by no means isolated cases. Tokenism most certainly
exists in the ranks of Australian management. As a woman manager
you face two enormous hurdles: the first set of stereotypes has to be
overcome in order to gain access to management, and then you have
to deal with the second set of stereotypical role expectations once
you are in. To succeed in this you certainly do have to be a 'superior'
performer.

SOME STRATEGIES FOR CHANGE

As stereotypes and role traps are not likely to disappear in the
immediate or even long-term future, what can you do? Is there a way
around these barriers, or does one just have to put up with them?
Will you always be 'not one of us'?

Well, you could wait until aspiring women managers are sufficiently strong in numbers to literally storm the bastion. However,
before that momentous occasion arises, you may be retired from the
workforce or have given up the struggle. Or you can accept the
situation as given and do nothing—just continue as usual, being
grateful for the little 'crumbs' that come your way.

Or you can adopt some strategies which may help you to achieve
the desired social change more quickly. Of course, inherent in these
strategies are some unpalatable 'truths' which have to be faced if
women are going to reach senior management.

First you must realise that you still face the same attitudinal barriers
of a decade or more ago. In fact, these barriers are likely to become
even more impenetrable in the future (despite Equal Employment
Opportunity and Affirmative Action) because of the pressures being
created by the increasing number of women wishing to pursue a
management career. Evidence of this resistance has been found in
the *Women in Management Study*.

Also, many younger women's expectations are unrealistic. Nur-
tured by the women's movement and the more recent legislative
changes, they believe that access to certain positions is almost gua-
ranteed. While many may achieve these posts (after all, the situation
is considerably more fluid than in the past), they are unprepared for
the attitudinal resistance which will prevent them from operating
effectively. The new generation of women managers needs to recognise that the attitudinal battle has not yet really been confronted.

Women's groups could assist new women managers by providing educational programmes on the types of attitudes they will come up against. The focus should no longer be on trying to get women into management: it should now be on facing the realities of the situation once they are in. That can only be achieved if women, as a group, realise they need support and guidance in surmounting the problems they face. Recognition of the problem is the first strategic step: a reality that has not yet been fully acknowledged in Australia.

The second strategic step is to recognise that you can assist attitudinal change once you have gained access to a certain level of management. An example is the woman marketing research manager who, together with her female colleagues, has embarked on a campaign to break down some of the resistance she has observed (quoted on pp. 35–6). However, this type of strategy depends on, women trusting each other and being prepared to cooperate. Such cooperation exists amongst the male managerial culture—why not amongst women managers? Fundamentally, this strategy works only within a single organisation. But if sufficient numbers of women adopted it, social change could be accelerated in the most important arena—the workplace.

Again, the women's literature needs to give prominence to these attitudinal issues. If attitudinal resistance exists, child-care or taxation relief for employment of nannies will not be enough. The *Women in Management Study* suggested that women were looking for guidance in this area. They were not finding it from *The Australian Woman's Weekly, Cleo, Cosmopolitan, Portfolio*, or the women's movement.

Finally, if women managers wish to be treated as serious contenders and not just tokens, they need to make a concerted effort to market themselves and their achievements. New role models need to be established and publicised. More research needs to be undertaken into the way women operate as managers. New training courses need to be established to enable women to understand the vicissitudes of management and the male managerial culture.

At the same time, the male managerial hierarchy needs to be encouraged to appreciate the problems faced by both men *and* women managers. At present women seem to be gathering in 'ghettos' for support and sustenance. Part of this appears to stem from the backlash already being experienced in some quarters. However, little progress will occur until the majority of male managers is involved. As men managers seem bewildered by the changes around them, women could help them to understand their reactions and to appreciate that men and women can both contribute to the management process.

WILL 'ENGINEERED' SOCIAL CHANGE BE QUICKER?

You may reject the strategies outlined above, believing that social change will only be achieved through the legislative process. But even this process will not induce the desired change or overcome all the attitudinal hurdles. Although the number of women in management may be increasing, they are not yet progressing up the hierarchy. Instead, they are accumulating in the lower levels of organisations—the graphs show it as a bulge.[31,32] However, employers will be able to claim to the Affirmative Action Agency (the new body created under the Affirmative Action [Equal Employment Opportunity for Women] Bill [1986]), that they are increasing the opportunities for women (after all, if you have one woman manager and employ another, you have increased your percentage by 100). However, while legislative change will ensure that organisations comply with the law and provide opportunities for women, it won't ensure that they will be either accepted or given the opportunities they desire. That battle remains to be fought internally, and by individual women.

Moreover, the peak employer groups are not exactly overjoyed with the prospect of Affirmative Action. In fact, the Business Council of Australia has registered its protest publicly:

> The Business Council, and business generally, does not support the extension of government through mandatory affirmative action programs. We believe that people of goodwill will achieve positive social change more effectively without regulatory intervention, and that such intervention can be counter-productive.[33]

The Confederation of Australian Industry (CAI) has similar views: 'Affirmative action legislation is unnecessary, undesirable, will add to employers' costs and will have counter-productive effects'.[34]

So, despite legislation, not everyone is enthusiastic about 'engineered' social change. It is important for you to realise that the attitudinal barriers will persist. Neither will loud cries of 'discrimination' win you any 'brownie points'. In fact, you will just turn everyone off. A concerted effort to work out how the attitudinal barriers can be effectively dealt with may do more for your cause than any amount of legislation or anti-discrimination action. You may never become 'one of us', but you will have reached your objective and fulfilled your career aspirations.

4

Fitting the managerial 'mould'

TO REACH SENIOR management you must learn to present an effective 'operating' style. This not only concerns the way you perform, but also how you present yourself as a manager, especially when dealing with others. The male managerial culture has several such operating styles. However, no acceptable general female management style exists, let alone one for top female executives. The male models prevail with most women adapting their behaviour to these standards.

The preferred male operating style has been established mainly through books and films. Current management books such as *In Search of Excellence,*[1] *The One Minute Manager*[2] and *Iococca—His Story,*[3] lay down the principles of successful management—male style. Rarely is a successful woman, or her style, featured this way, probably because of the lack of female managerial achievers. Women's books like *The Business Amazons*[4] and *Targeting Success: From a Woman's Point of View*[5] deal mainly with female issues—for instance, 'how to find time to study while raising a family' and 'getting

39

the family to accept their changed life style once you go to work'. While these are important issues, and require a solution, they do not necessarily prepare women for management or its daily operating problems. Faced with a lack of alternative models, then, women managers have little choice. The only message they receive is that they should adopt the masculine version of style in order to survive in the management world or be locked out of the arenas of power and decision-making.

THE 'MOULD'

Given that women have no real behavioural choice if they wish to reach senior management, what is the model they must conform to? There is no one ready description of the 'accepted' male managerial style. However, observation reveals it to be a mixture of the following behaviour and 'image' factors which are believed to distinguish successful from unsuccessful managers:

■ Successful and effective managers project an aura which suggests that they are in total command of the situation. Displays of temperament or emotion are non-existent, as are indications of insecurity. Any deviation from this norm is considered to be sign of weakness and leaves the executive vulnerable to attack.

■ Successful managers also present a particular image, which revolves around the way they dress, the suburbs they live in, the cars they drive, the schools their children attend, the friends/associates they entertain, and the trappings of the executive's own office environment. A conservative image prevails, both in respect to the sombre business attire and the 'blue-chip' schools, suburbs, friends and cars. The overall impression is one of class, dignity, taste, refinement and understated luxury. These factors signal that the executive has 'arrived' and is considered a 'leader' in the managerial world.

■ Successful managers also exhibit a particular 'social style'. Executives who have it are usually urbane, suave, softly spoken, and have a quick but light sense of humour. They are courteous and especially sensitive to the impact of their words and actions on others. Executives without this style exhibit a reverse form of behaviour. Loud, aggressive, egotistical, insensitive and 'crude', they offend rather than win support. Their 'bulldozing' techniques may get results, but they are not considered effective managers. Consequently, they rarely achieve senior management positions unless they are entrepreneurs or own the company.

■ Finally, successful managers exhibit an 'operating' style which marks them out as being self-reliant, independent, aggressive and dominant. They are decisive, know where they are going, take risks (or give the impression of doing so), thrive on competition, and can be ruthless when the occasion demands ('It's business you know'). Their style gives them the aura of the 'gung-ho operator'—one who is destined for success.

Women, however, are not perceived to 'fit' this mould. The myths and stereotypes discussed in chapter 3 not only prevent women from being appointed to management, they also impinge upon the perceptions of a woman's 'operating style' if she does become a manager. Generally, the stereotypes portray a woman's way of managing as the very antithesis of the preferred model. Consider these 'known' effects on a woman's perceived management style:

■ Women are 'known' to be submissive, dependent, non-combative, non-competitive, sensitive, gentle and yielding. As these qualities are not considered to be the hallmark of 'good' and 'effective' managers, women tend to be considered unsuitable for management.

■ Women are also 'known' to be 'emotional', especially at their 'time of the month'. This means that they will be unreliable in times of stress and subject to outbursts of temperament. Tears and hysteria will be the order of the day when the 'going gets tough'. Neither of these 'traits' is also considered to be suitable for management.

■ Women are also 'known' to be incapable of 'making hard decisions' and 'understanding the bottom line'. Consequently, they will not earn the respect of either their peers or their subordinates. Place them in a negotiating role with an outside competitor or supplier and the company will have to suffer the consequences. Women just 'don't know what to do' and are likely to be unpredictable at these crucial times.

■ Women are also 'known' to be more family-oriented than career-oriented. Invest money in a woman's progress and she is likely to repay the organisation by leaving to have a baby. She will also want to take her leave to coincide with school holidays, and will always be missing when the children are sick. From time to time shopping trips, dental appointments, paying bills and collecting the dry-cleaning will also require her undivided attention. When the organisation wants her she will not be available because of her 'female' responsibilities.

If it all sounds familiar it is because these arguments are so frequently used to prove that women should not be in management. They are also used to bolster the notion that the male managerial model is the only one with credibility and legitimacy. Because women are considered to be unpredictable, erratic and emotional it is felt that business could not operate under such leadership styles. Therefore, if organisations are to be ensured of continuation the male managerial model is the only acceptable version.

CONSEQUENCES OF FITTING THE 'MOULD'

If you decide to give in to the inevitable and accept the male managerial model as your role guide, what limitations does this place upon you as a woman manager?

For a start, adoption of the male managerial model of style locks you into a rather unnatural behaviour pattern. Think of those successful women who appear before the general public via the media. Each displays a calm and rational demeanour, hiding any traces of panic or hysteria. The same 'face' is always presented to the public no matter the situation, in case the woman is criticised for not being able to handle responsibility. In attempting to emulate the accepted management style, she is perceived to be 'hard, calculating and less than human'. Her own personal behavioural style becomes subservient to the model of 'correct' behaviour.

Diana, aged 42, and a senior manager in a financial institution describes the situation as follows:

> I just think the whole scene is unfair to women. Whenever I go to meetings I just have to sit there and be calm and serene while all the guys can be literally throwing tantrums and 'tearing their hair out'. It is perfectly acceptable for them to do this. They feel that they are entitled to 'let their hair down' because they have been under pressure. Poor things! If I did it—and I must admit there are times when I feel like lashing out—I would be branded as a hysterical female and one who could not be trusted to make

responsible decisions regarding investment. One slip and I would lose all credibility. I don't see why a woman can't behave normally, but it is just not allowed. I have to save my 'tantrums' or feelings of displeasure or frustration until I go home.

Diana's description of male emotional behaviour may seem strange especially when the 'ideal' managerial image abhors such displays of emotion. However, observations of organisational life reveal such incidents to be a fact of life. An occasional male tempermental 'outbreak' is accepted in the male managerial culture. However, such licence is not given to the woman executive. To survive in the power structure, she must at all times conform to the idealised model. This enables her colleagues to interact with her. Men are used to displays of emotion from women at home. They just cannot cope when this emotion is transferred to the workplace. The woman thus sacrifices her individual personality and adopts male behaviour patterns— minus the emotion.

The managerial 'mould' also requires that you try to inhibit any overt signs of femininity. This applies particularly to the way you dress. A whole fashion industry has evolved to cater for the 'career' woman. Generally the fashions favoured are a poor imitation of male business attire. Neutral or sombre colours, severely tailored styles, 'neck to knee' coverage and little individuality. The object is to present a non-threatening and sexless image in order to be accepted as a credible person.

Eve, aged 54, and a senior woman consultant with extensive overseas management experience, explains her ready adoption of the dress code:

I always ensure that whenever I go out to visit a male client, be they young or old, that I dress either in black or white. I don't wear any makeup and I try not to have any colour about me at all—not even lipstick. That way I ensure that I am completely neutral and don't stand out in any way—I just merge into the background. The clients then forget that I am a woman—there is nothing about me to distract them. We can then get down to business. I have found this to be a very successful technique when I am negotiating. I am not there to compete with the men—I want the contract.

Of course you may not need to go to such extremes, especially if you work in fashion or advertising. However, Eve's case illustrates the pressures that women face from the male managerial model. A major restriction is the denial of their feminine qualities in order to be treated as a serious person.

A third limitation concerns accepted male 'social' behaviour. Women managers find that they are at a disadvantage in establishing 'contacts' because they do not have the same opportunities to join in weekly drinking sessions with the 'boys', go sailing or golfing on a regular basis with clients, or have a drink after hours with a male colleague. Social mores have not yet progressed sufficiently to allow the woman manager the same social latitude as her male counterpart.

Margaret, 47, and owner of her own business, explains:

> There is no doubt that I am at a disadvantage compared to my competitors. It all has to do with this male sport thing. They can go sailing or golfing with the clients — in fact, one chap I know does this regularly every week. He has a standing arrangement with the Managing Director. It's the same with entertaining. The men can go drinking each night or on Friday — a woman cannot. She's virtually locked out of these social circles and if she tries to enter them the sex aspect rears its head. You know: 'What's going on here? Perhaps she fancies me'. Men now accept that a woman can take them to lunch without there being sexual overtones. But after hours—no way! The only way that I can see a woman overcoming these hurdles is to be that much more professional than her competitors. You can't compete on the other social grounds.

Interestingly, a similar restriction applies to men in their interaction with women. An English manager, Len Cardwell, supports Margaret's comments:

> *Taking a Woman to Lunch*
> Once my new-found confidence was established I concluded that, as I had many work conversations with male colleagues in the pub, there must be no harm in discussing business with a woman in the same place. *Wrong.* My wife was the first to remind me that there are intrinsic differences between men and women. The old adage that a woman cannot be seen drinking alone in a pub may be supplemented with the addition that a man cannot be seen drinking with a single woman in the pub. In this respect doing it twice is evidence of a relationship. In the eyes of the world the relationship between manager and managed is of secondary importance.
> I have it on good authority that the reverse is also problematical. There is a breed of man who refuses to allow a woman to buy him a drink. In essence he is refusing to treat the woman as a colleague; he is only concerned with her sexuality. It would appear that my wife shares this narrow view of office relationships.[6]

Of course not every woman has to contend with this type of limitation. But if women are interested in furthering their business interests, then socialising is part of the scene. It is considered to be a congenial way of trading and reaching agreement. Unfortunately, the ground rules have been established by the male managerial culture. The woman manager has to find ways of counteracting these disadvantages because *she* is the late entrant to management, not her male peers.

A fourth effect of the accepted managerial style is that women managers are almost forced to be 'superwomen'. Because they are constantly reminded of the virtues and standards of the idealised effective manager, they endeavour to overachieve in order to meet the image requirements. This overachievement can take several forms:

■ The woman manager 'lives' the job: works long hours, has little social life, foregoes marriage or family responsibilities, is always available for business and professional activities.

■ She attempts to combine career, marriage and family at the same level of intensity. Childbearing becomes an automatic event, along with overseas trips, home entertaining, and the occasional media appearance. Seen at all the best social and cultural events, her daily activities are timed to the split second. She is never ill; she just keeps adding activities to her already overcrowded schedule.

■ She attempts a distance dual career (in which each partner works in a different state or country) and is usually separated from her home and family. Weekend visits home become part of her routine. This ritual may go on for years—either until a new position is attained or the marriage splits. The job becomes the objective and all other aspects of her life are surrendered to this.

The first two forms of overachievement are easily recognised. However, the third form is newly emerging in the managerial world. Consider the case of Ruth, 36, and Managing Director of a large division of a multi-national company:

My marriage has recently ended and I put this down to the fact that I really sacrificed it to my career. It was all right in the early days when we were travelling the world for his career. But then I got a job, just out of sheer boredom. Before I knew where I was the job had taken off and I was offered a management opportunity in another country in Europe. We discussed it and decided to let me have my chance. We really lived apart for three years with the exception of the monthly weekend. Either I would fly to him or he would come to me. At first we tried to get together much more often but business began to intervene and our times together became more infrequent. Eventually I was offered a job here in Australia. I asked him if he was prepared to put his career on 'hold' so that we could come to this country and perhaps be together more. He agreed, but as you can see it hasn't worked out. He was able to continue his career as before. However, mine really took off and I had to keep leaving him to go overseas. He just found someone else. The other woman does not have a career.

Not all dual career arrangements end in this fashion. However, Ruth's case illustrates the dilemma of a married woman manager. Whose career should take precedence: hers or her partner's? In previous times the man's career was the guiding force in the family unit. With the increasing right of women to a career, this practice is being challenged. The male managerial model also adds its pressures. If women wish to be considered for promotion, and as serious contenders in the management arena, they must be prepared to travel, move interstate or even overseas. Their personal lives have to be sacrificed to meet the demands of their job and organisation. Men have long made those sacrifices. The same pressures are now being placed upon women. The only problem is that they still have to be wives and mothers. Not all men are prepared to assist a wife in her career. In general the woman's career will take second place and her opportunities for advancement will be limited.

The accepted managerial style thus has some serious pitfalls for women managers. While some women are overcoming them, the great majority still faces these barriers. There seems to be no one solution. While the male style prevails in the managerial world, women will be required to adjust in return for experience and a chance to prove themselves. The price seems high. However, it will continue to be extracted until more women enter management and become equal partners in the decision-making process.

AUSTRALIAN MANAGEMENT STYLE—MALE AND FEMALE

What does the research tell us about how men and women operate as managers in this country? Do they act the same, or are there differences in the way they manage despite the 'mould'?

Table 4.1 shows that the overwhelming majority of the 1093 Australians in the *Women in Management Study* believe that men and women managers vary in their management style. This view was expressed by all six research groups, whether managers, future managers or non-managers, and most strongly by women managers and non-managers.

Interestingly, many favourable comments were expressed about women's management style. Consider the following:

- Women try harder to gain the respect and cooperation of their subordinates (particularly men subordinates), whereas male bosses turn to 'verbal aggression' to cut through difficult subordinates. *Male non-manager, aged 30*

- Women have a tendency to be more sensitive to the needs of subordinates, probably because of their past experiences. *Male non-manager, 33*

- Women are more professional, consult people more, better at getting support for decisions. *Male manager, 34*

- Women spend more time on detail. *Male manager, 37*

- Women are more perceptive of and more in tune with the needs of others in the workplace and less likely to make hard-headed, calculated decisions without putting everything in perspective and considering all aspects first. *Woman manager, 30*

- Women are more conciliatory and less confrontational—more thorough and inspirational. *Woman non-manager, 50*

- My former superior (a woman) led by example with inspiration, fairness and compassion in a very positive manner, as opposed to the many power games my male superiors play. I developed and grew more in a non-sexist, non-patronising and non-aggressive environment than in any other position, both before and since. *Woman manager, 38*

However, despite these encouraging remarks, some negative aspects to women's management style were noted. Generally these aspects have a stereotypical flavour. For example:

- Women lack the aggressive attitude needed to be a leader. They tend to have hang-ups on ability (confidence). *Male non-manager, 46*

Table 4.1   Do the management styles of men differ from the management styles of women?

Response	Total group	Men managers	Women managers	Men students	Women students	Men non-managers	Women non-managers
Styles differ	711 (65.1)	157 (66.8)	146 (73.8)	158 (61.5)	97 (61.4)	51 (50.5)	102 (70.8)
No difference	311 (28.4)	66 (28.0)	43 (21.7)	75 (29.2)	49 (31.0)	42 (41.6)	36 (25.0)
Undecided	27 (2.5)	6 (2.6)	6 (3.0)	4 (1.5)	2 (1.3)	5 (4.9)	4 (2.8)
No response	44 (4.0)	6 (2.6)	3 (1.5)	20 (7.8)	10 (6.3)	3 (3.0)	2 (1.4)
Total	1093	235	198	257	158	101	144

- Women are emotional, and their management styles are not systematic. *Male non-manager, 36*

- The differences are mainly due to personality differences. However, women tend to be more serious, less humorous, still grappling with trying to be super executives, super mum, world's greatest lover, etc. *Woman manager, 27*

- Women try to be too authoritarian to make up for lack of confidence. They do not delegate effectively. *Woman manager, 30*

- Women can be very finicky over unimportant detail. *Woman non-manager, 56*

- Women are inflexible and often expect situations to fall within their pre-determined expectations. *Male student, 23*

- Women lack flexibility and are gung-ho—like everyone had to be as good as they are. *Male student, 26*

Women were, however, recognised as having a number of qualities that are apparently appreciated by their subordinates. They are seen as being humane, considerate, understanding of people and appreciative of individual differences. None of these qualities were acknowledged in male managers, a definite plus for women managers—especially those aiming for senior positions.

Apparently it is the unpredictable and 'female' elements in women's nature which makes some people dislike them as managers. For instance, their fussiness, 'bitchiness' or 'cattiness', overreaction to power because of prior socialisation, and inexperience.

The message is obvious if you wish to become a top woman manager. You should endeavour to capitalise on your strengths and minimise your weaknesses. While some people may argue that this is unfair in today's climate of equal opportunity and anti-discrimination, the fact is that women managers still face an accceptance problem. The style question reveals some reasons why and also suggests some answers to this perennial problem.

How do men's and women's management styles compare to that of the 'ideal' manager? The 1093 Australians depicted men's, women's and the ideal manager's style as shown in Table 4.2, from a list of 38 style descriptions.

Interestingly, there is a lot of agreement between the three profiles. Moreover, the woman manager's style profile has 80 per cent correspondence with that of the ideal manager, while the male man-

Table 4.2 Male, female and ideal management styles

Male management style	Female management style	Ideal management style
self-confident	competent	competent
competent	determined	knowledgeable
knowledgeable	self-confident	dependable
determined	knowledgeable	innovative
competitive	thorough	self-confident
aggressive	dependable	logical
logical	competitive	honest
dependable	innovative	fair
enterprising	logical	thorough
firm	honest	friendly

ager's profile only has 50 per cent correspondence with that of the ideal manager.

Before you become too heartened by this interesting development, compare the variations between profiles. Male managers are considered to be aggressive, enterprising and firm while women are not. On the other hand, women managers are portrayed as thorough, innovative and honest, while men are not. Neither men nor women managers are perceived to be fair or friendly, two qualities valued in the ideal manager.

Many people saw no differences in style between men and women managers, giving both genders the same style descriptions. However, most perceived a style difference.

Despite this encouraging news, the lack of an accepted management style does tend to go against women. Because they are not sure how to behave, they can adopt an inappropriate style. This can have a major effect on their careers. In case you still have some doubts about how this can occur, contemplate the not unusual case of Dorothy, who after many years is still struggling to get accepted and promoted to a senior job. Her main fault: an abrasive style:

> I just don't know what I am going to do. I just can't change my personality. No matter what I do, or how hard I try to dampen it down the odds still go against me. I only have to open my mouth and people see me as loud-mouthed, aggressive, domineering and abrasive. I'm sure it's because I am a big person and I laugh loudly. And why not? I enjoy life (which is more than my detractors

do). But it is going against me now. Once it didn't matter, but now I'm at the age where I still want to reach the top and I don't get the jobs because of my so-called 'abrasive personality'.

For instance, the other day I was on the short list for this very senior job and I felt confident of the outcome. The interview went well, the atmosphere was good, and my qualifications and experience matched what they were looking for. Then they said they would do a further reference check — one apart from the referees I had given them. My heart sank because I knew that if they checked in certain sections at work I was already labelled with this 'abrasive' reputation. Sure enough. It seems I struck out again. I didn't hear anything from them so I rang to find the outcome of the interview. The person I spoke to was suddenly evasive, and told me that while I had good experience etc., the job had gone to someone else who was more 'suitable'. Of course suitable wasn't defined even though I tried to find out why I had missed on the job. The person hung up quickly—he was very embarrassed. I think I will have to go to a charm school even at this late stage in my life because obviously I don't know what counts these days. Hard work and performance don't seem enough. You also have to market yourself in an acceptable way and personal style apparently counts more than some of the other criteria!

Given that women still lack an effective 'operating' style, which do most people prefer for a boss—a man or a woman? Table 4.3 illustrates the choice of 1093 Australians.

Most Australians apparently prefer a male to be their boss. This preference is strongest among the three male groups and the women non-managers. The women managers and the women future managers (students) are less sure, with 34 per cent of the women managers being unable to make a choice. It is to be hoped such ambivalence does not extend to other areas of their decision-making!

Typical reasons given for preferring the male are:

- It is easier to settle an argument with a male boss. *Male non-manager, aged 65*

- There is more chance of finding common ground with a 'bad' male boss than a 'bad' female boss if you are male. *Male non-manager, 30*

- A male boss appears to be easier to get along with, less difficult to offend and on the whole less moody than a female. *Male non-manager, 28*

Table 4.3 Which do you prefer as a boss?

Preference	Total group	Men managers	Women managers	Men students	Women students	Men non-managers	Women non-managers
A man	566 (51.8)	161 (68.5)	61 (30.8)	151 (58.7)	65 (41.2)	56 (55.4)	72 (50.0)
A woman	204 (18.7)	18 (7.7)	43 (21.7)	50 (19.4)	37 (23.4)	13 (12.9)	43 (29.9)
Indifferent	88 (8.0)	4 (1.7)	14 (7.1)	11 (4.3)	9 (5.7)	27 (26.7)	23 (16.0)
Undecided	155 (14.2)	41 (17.4)	67 (33.8)	22 (8.6)	18 (11.4)	2 (2.0)	5 (3.4)
No response	80 (7.3)	11 (4.7)	13 (6.6)	23 (9.0)	29 (18.3)	3 (3.0)	1 (0.7)
Total	1093	235	198	257	158	101	144

- I have been brought up in an all male business environment. My difficulty would be to take orders from a woman—it rankles. *Male manager, 36*

- I relate more easily to the opposite sex (where the person is in a higher power position). Besides I consider that I would become competitive against another woman in a managerial position. With a male manager I would consider myself his equal, but with differences existing between us. *Woman manager, 43*

- There is less cattiness or talk behind your back when the boss is a male. *Woman future manager, 22*

- I personally find it easier to take orders from men, and working women with school age children annoy me. *Woman non-manager, 29*

- I have found a lot of women when they reach these high positions seem to thrive on the power they have over you, whereas many men just take it in their stride and are usually more approachable—maybe it is just that opposite sexes have that unexplainable something which isn't there when a woman employee has a woman boss. *Woman non-manager, 26*

One of the main reasons given by people who prefer a male boss is that men know how to be aggressive and assertive and women don't. In the public's mind aggression and assertiveness coincide with dominance and authority. Women are not considered to be such 'effective' managers as men because they 'lack' these desirable qualities.

However, some people hold the contrary view that women in authority are too aggressive, and it seems that subordinates are repelled by such aggressiveness.

Two studies have recently shown that Australian women managers are quite assertive.[7] In the first study they were found to be more assertive than men and women of the general population—that is, non-managers. In the second, there were no significant differences in expressed assertiveness levels between 137 men and 115 women managers.

Perhaps an extreme example of how assertive women managers sometimes need to be is the story of Barbara, aged 58, managing director of a transport company:

I find that you have to stand up to men and then you don't have any opposition. If you come back at them when they attack you, and then attack again when they retaliate, they just can't cope with this and usually leave you alone. You have to be firm. Let me give you an illustration.

One day my second-in-charge and I went to collect a bad debt—my company was owed $20 000. We went out in my old pick-up truck to the yard of the company which owed us the money. I went to find the owner and before I could do anything a group of men with 'two by four's' in their hands advanced towards me and my second-in-charge. It looked as if they were going 'to do us over'. I decided to take a stand, so walked over to the truck *calmly* and casually picked up a rifle from the front seat and pointed it at them (having taken the precaution to take it with me in the first place). You couldn't see their heels for dust! Needless to say, I got the money that was owing. It might sound like I was trying to be Annie Oakley, but sometimes you have to take such measures.

Women bosses were preferred by 20 per cent of the 1093 Australians—mainly the women managers, future managers and non-managers. Their preference tended to respect the 'female' characteristics of women (a trend which also emerged in the above discussion on style). For example:

- A woman is more understanding, harder working, more fun (sense of humour), tougher when it comes to making important decisions—men act tough but often go soft when it comes to the crunch. *Male manager, 34*

- Women have sensitivity, and there is less inter-male conflict/ assertiveness, or 'ego clash'. *Male manager 25*

- As a male I find women generally more rational and clear thinking in managerial positions. Also they appear to be less threatened by ambitious young men than male managers are. *Male manager, 37*

- I can get closer to a woman boss. I happen to be a bit unsure of myself with men. I don't know how to handle any advances that are unwelcome or unwise. *Woman non-manager, 50*

- The majority of male superiors are not fully *aware* of what a capable female can achieve, or give them an opportunity to do so. Men are always constantly thinking of *the* female/male interaction, which I feel inhibits your work style. *Woman manager, 26*

Some men actually like working for a woman. Consider how Barbara's second-in-charge sums her up:

> I find there is no difference in working for Barbara or a man. I've worked for some real bastards in my time. Barbara is as good as a man—there's no difference. The only thing she can't do is change tyres on trucks, and I feel that there are plenty of men around here to do that—she doesn't have to do it. We've been together seven years now, and I can tell her moods—everything about her. We don't even need to communicate. I sit in the front here and she sits at the back. I can see her face in that mirror on the wall. She only has to raise an eyebrow and I know what the temperature is like. But that's okay. She has a lot of problems to contend with in this job. But the guys here all like working for her. Most of them have been with the company since it started fourteen years ago. In fact, they get Barbara to defend them against their wives—you know, if they have a late night out on the town. They ask her to explain to the wife what has happened.
>
> We have some funny times here too when new people come to the office. Because people see me first, where a girl should sit, they think I am the boss. Then I tell them to go into the next room and they find Barbara. You should see the look on their faces! It's a real role reversal!

It is nice to know that we have supporters! However, women still have to face the fact that men are preferred as managers. This does not mean that you have to turn tail and run. It just means that you do not fit in with custom and tradition.

IS ANDROGYNY THE ANSWER?

Would you be better accepted if you adopted an androgynous management style? Androgyny is currently being promoted as the 'new' management style—for both men and women. While people may complain about women, they are also very caustic about the inhumaneness of men!

Androgyny highlights the fact that people have both masculine and feminine qualities. An androgynous style is considered to be a balanced one, and an answer to the extremes of masculinity and femininity in the workplace.[8] The style incorporates the Chinese concepts of yin and yang. Leaders and managers who embrace this style use both logic and intuition, recognise both facts and feelings, and are both technically competent and emotionally caring. The 'new' manager is '. . . a kind of managerial mutant, a new corporate type, the gamesman who develops his heart as well as his head, and who could thus become an example for leadership in a changing society where the goal is economic democracy and the humanisation of technology'.[9]

Androgyny is said to answer women's management acceptance problem because they possess the desired feminine qualities of the model. However, research findings are mixed. Some subordinates find an androgynous style very acceptable in women.[10] Alternatively, others indicate that it is more advantageous for men and women to possess 'masculine' qualities because 'feminine' qualities are not perceived to coincide with the achievement and retention of power.[11,12,13,14] As Hester Eisenstein puts it:

> The androgynous ideal [appears] to ignore or to gloss over issues of power. It [holds] out a promise of social change via individual psychological transformation. There [is] no room in the androgyny concept for market forces or other material factors. And there certainly [is] little or no acknowledgement of the political dimension of relations between men and women.[15]

There appears to be no clear answer to the dilemma: should you or shouldn't you adopt this style? If anything androgyny is a 'softer' version of the male managerial style, to introduce men to the more human needs of their employees. However, it does not necessarily offer an 'open sesame' for women. While feminine qualities are valued in women managers, androgyny still does not provide the perfect solution to their acceptance problem.

THE DILEMMA: WHAT TO DO?

If androgyny is not the 'magic' answer, what do you do to improve your management prospects?

Well, like it or not, you could develop some 'masculine' type characteristics. No matter how you feel about this prospect, aggression, competitiveness and leadership are still valued in management. The current crop of assertiveness training courses attempt to develop these skills in women. If you feel that you are deficient in some way, take a course. There are plenty, ranging from private therapy groups, to management consultants, to those run by the Directorate of Equal Opportunity in Public Employment (DEOPE).

Assertiveness training aims to assist women who are perceived to be passive, weak, compliant, indecisive, easily moved to tears, susceptible to suggestion from others, or easily led and persuaded.[16]

It endeavours to help women overcome their constant need to be a nurturer, compassionate or tender, and to acquire the more valued 'masculine' qualities of aggressiveness, leadership, initiative and competitiveness. Every effort is made to help women 'stand up' and defend themselves—but in a socially acceptable way. So try it and see. You may be surprised at how such a course can help enhance your career.

If this suggestion does not appeal to you, then you will just have to be like Jane in Chapter 3 (pp. 35–6) and attempt to get your male counterparts to both work with you and like you. Some progressive firms are recognising that men and women managers have to be trained together to break down some of the barriers. However, if you are not in this enviable situation the alternative will have to do. As Pedler and Fritchie explain:

> Male managers are used to working *with* other men, and to having women work *for* them so the increasing number of women in work (including the few who get through into management) creates situations in which everybody may feel uneasy. Men find it difficult to act appropriately towards women as colleagues, there is little knowledge of how men and women should work together.[17]

The advent of affirmative action means that men will have to learn to work with women—mainly because more women will be given a chance through the removal of discriminatory barriers. Some firms are now giving their male executives management development training to enable them to appreciate the social changes. However, you can do a lot yourself if you recognise the nature of the problem. It is not that men don't like you. It is just that they are not used to having women around in the workplace, except in subordinate positions.

Of course, there is a third alternative. Feminist writers feel that women should develop a new style based on the strengths they have acquired throughout their historic oppression. The qualities that they have had to develop—that is, their 'ability to express vulnerability, weakness and helplessness; their capacity to experience, express, and interpret emotions; their capacity to cultivate cooperativeness, and to encourage coordination and working together'[18]—should become the building blocks of a new and more humane organisational culture.

While this 'new woman produced by feminism' has its appealing qualities, the fact remains that 'new style' managers must cope with 'old style' management structures.

Take heart. Women are moving into management, albeit slowly.

The real reason you are not accepted in management, or do not have the correct operating style, is that men don't wish to share *power*. They have to have some place where they can play their games, and that is the workplace. Hence, they will do everything they can to stop the invasion—including saying that you do not fit the mould. So forget about the fact that you are not accepted, or don't 'operate' as well as they do. These are just red herrings and excuses to stop you from entering their domain. What you really have to do is to understand the power plays for what they are. If you can do that, then you will really be on your way to being a success!

THE LAST TABOO: POWER AND YOU

If you truly wish to be a top woman manager and want to fit the 'mould', then you must learn how to grasp and handle power.

Power comes with leadership and management, although it may also come from expert knowledge or attachments to other powerful figures. Men have traditionally had the most power in organisations, largely because so few women have been in positions of authority. Those women that have been in management have usually managed powerless people, such as clerical workers.[19] Moreover, women managers have not generally been recognised as powerful, primarily because of their 'fringe' and specialist, rather than mainstream, roles.

Can women handle power? There is no evidence to the contrary, especially with role models like Mrs Thatcher and the late Indira Gandhi.

Do women seek power? This is less clear, mainly because of the lack of women managers or women in significantly visible roles. However, if you are a student of history and have read the stories of prominent women it would appear that power is certainly sought by some women.

Some women, like some men, seek power for its own sake, which can be very destructive. Consider the case of Janice, aged 38, who was on the receiving end of another woman's ambitions for power:

> I first became aware that this subordinate was out to 'get' me when she invited me to lunch. I didn't want to go, but she had a bad reputation in the company and I thought it would be prudent if I did. I didn't know what the purpose was, and was relieved when the event passed pleasantly. She was on her best behaviour, I on mine, and all in all it didn't reveal anything startling.
>
> Her next move came a couple of weeks later. This time it was

another lunch, but with four other women. I was 'trapped' into going, mainly because it was a farewell lunch. This time, however, I began to feel uneasy and left as soon as I could.

About a week after this she came to my office to see me on a minor matter. The discussion developed into an argument, mainly because we were both talking at cross purposes. The misunderstanding did not become clear until almost at the end of our discussion. During the course of it, she made several allegations about something I was involved in and when I questioned her about them she began to make all sorts of comments about how stupid I was, how I didn't understand how organisations worked, that she had all the alliances in the place, and that she and her 'friends' could remove me at any time if they so desired. Despite this unpleasantness I believed that we parted on fairly equitable terms.

Two days later the union requested that I be removed from my position because I had no integrity and was prejudicial to this particular woman. They claimed I had intimidated her in a very heated discussion, had been acrimonious, she was terribly upset and I was not fit to be in charge.

I immediately understood what was happening. She had boasted to me that she knew how the system worked, and she did. She was working the anti-discrimination legislation against me and trying to prove a case for discrimination.

The trouble was that her story was believed because everyone was frightened of her. I had walked into the situation with my eyes open. It was a trumped up charge, but she held all the aces. She had also boasted to me that she was after power. Apparently she is determined to get it the easy way by taking over my job.

Women managers have to learn to face such situations when they arise. Janice's case was unusual because it involved another woman —not a man. Usually, such power plays occur between men and women, especially if the woman is the boss. Men are just not used to taking orders from a woman and will try everything they know to 'go around' her to the more senior people. There is no such thing as hierarchy or management principles when men are seeking power. The woman is just in the way, and the men will make this obvious to all.

Margaret is continually facing this problem with one of her male subordinates:

No matter what I do this chap will just not accept me as his boss. I have had several discussions with him to point out the 'error' of his ways, and he just blandly sits there and ignores what I say. He runs his department okay. What he does is make all his requests to my boss and not to me. Usually I don't even find out about it until the boss rings me up and asks my opinion. I never get a copy of the letter. Of course my boss is in error too because he should just tell him that he reports to me and that's that. I think men like to stick together in these matters. It makes them feel big and they can then down the 'little woman'. My subordinate just refuses to report to me because I am a woman. The tragedy is that I picked him for the job. Doesn't say much for my judgement, does it?

To be a top woman manager you will have to overcome resentments such as these. Most women managers have at least one subordinate who will not accept them. Not all are so blatant about it as in Margaret's situation. It is important that you realise that you are likely to have such problems. The unfortunate thing is that, like Margaret, you can't always fire the transgressor. So try to be on good terms with the boss, if only to protect your rear position.

Of course, if you handle power well it will make you out as a true 'operator', one who is destined for senior positions. Smart operators do it with style and panache. Some people establish a personality cult to show others that they have power. Indicators are that they always travel first class, have a Rolls Royce, can dispense favours at the drop of the hat, and so on. Others try to hide their power because it can have unpleasant side effects, like always being expected to do something for others, give money, and be a 'soft touch'.

However, as a woman it would be very difficult for you to avoid the trappings of power. You are just so visible in the corporate world that you might as well enjoy it. So get the smart office, the scenic view, the apartment, and act the part. Just remember that once having gained power you can also lose it. Sometimes it is much harder to hang on to power than it is to attain it. You may also have to learn how to be *ruthless* in your exercise of power. That will truly mark you out as an 'operator', one who has conformed to the mould. You will have established yourself as a 'rising star'!

5

K nowing your career direction

YOU WILL BECOME a senior manager much faster if you have a clear career goal. This means that you know where you are going in your career. Successful people have usually aimed for a specific job within a specific time—such as Managing Director by the time they are 40. Others are less definite, but are strongly vertically oriented in their career aspirations. Few reach senior positions by letting life just 'happen' to them, or hoping that someone will rescue them from their drudgery or recognise their 'shining light under a bushel'. They achieve because they had an idea of what they would like to do and set out to do it!

People with clear career directions thus avoid jobs that just fill in time before marriage and children. They also avoid the 'interesting' jobs which give a great deal of 'job satisfaction' and where they feel they are 'contributing something worthwhile to society'—especially if these jobs lead nowhere. Instead, they aim for the jobs that have a future, that lead to the top of the management hierarchy.

CAREER GOALS — MALE AND FEMALE

Most women do not have a clear career goal. Conditioned by society to believe that marriage and motherhood is their 'real' career, they fill in time in the workplace until they can embark upon their true vocation. Consequently, those who work often either remain in the same job (called a stationary career), or they move around at the same level (called a lateral career). Few have a vertical career path—the pathway for the ambitious and career-minded—which aims *up* the hierarchy through promotion.

Men do not day-dream about careers. They know they are going to be in the workforce most of their lives. Only a few are invalided out with 'nerves' or become 'den mothers' while their wives take over as breadwinners. Given their long sentence, then, men generally take the short-cut. They just aim for the top—the vertical career. For those who are less ambitious, their male colleagues will 'look out for them' and help them along. You might have heard the story: 'Gee, Hal is such a nice guy. He's been going through a bad patch lately. Nothing seems to go right for him. And there is all that trouble at home. Let's give him a chance and promote him into this job.'

It is the rare woman who knows where she is going in her career. Interview them about their intentions, and a great many will reply. 'Oh. I didn't really have any ambitions. I started out doing this and that job when I left school because I wanted to travel overseas. Then someone suggested I ought to apply for such and such a job. I did, and found I liked the work. And it just seemed to develop from there. I don't know how I got here, but I do know I work hard and for long hours!'

The interesting consequence of such unstructured career aspirations is that many women feel they have to apologise for success as if it is 'unfeminine' to have achieved. They try to avoid being the 'tall poppy' especially in mixed company. Men labour under no such delusions. They expect homage and patronage and get it. After all, that is one of the rewards for reaching the top of the hierarchy. It is no good achieving, if no one acknowledges it!

These comments may seem unfair to women especially as they do not have the same lives as men—even in the workplace. As Westbrook and Nordholm explain:

> . . .the job model that has been applied to male careers treats men as uniform in their family situations. The gender model that has been applied to female careers treats women as differing in their

family situations, but uniform with relation to employment.
Moreover, the patterns of men's relations to employment are used
as the standard in the analysis of feminine careers.[1]

What this means is that women usually have interrupted career
paths through marriage and family, while men have uninterrupted
ones. Many women cannot embark upon a career until they complete
their childbearing and rearing days, and more often than not they
never catch up. They are judged, and found wanting, in terms of the
male career pattern, especially in terms of job continuity and
experience.

Interestingly, many women still don't appreciate that having job
continuity and experience is vital for a career. They feel that they
have a right to go in and out of the workforce at will according to their
needs and fancies. Employers do not hold the same views. They want
a worker who is going to think in terms of continuity and career. Many
women finding themselves in a situation where 'the boss doesn't like
me', or 'it's not a very friendly place to work', or 'it's too far to travel' or
'the job interferes with my private life', will choose to leave the job.
Such an attitude is seldom tolerated. Would-be achievers may just
have to accept that they have to plod along for some years gaining
the necessary 'continuity and experience' before earning the long-
desired promotion.

However, in these days of delayed families, dual-career families
and professional and career-minded women, the inherent discrimination in this male-designed job model is not always relevant. Women
are in the workforce to stay, and to have careers. They just have to
learn to distinguish between a job and a career. Many think their job
is their career. It may well turn out to be in the long run—through
chance rather than through design. But most women's jobs still lack a
vertical career path. Instead, they conform to the old pattern of
stationary and lateral career paths.

WHERE IS MY PIGEON HOLE?

Where are women establishing careers—either stationary, lateral or
vertical? The *Women in Management Study* found significant numbers in marketing, personnel, advertising, public relations, some areas
of accounting, and office administration. In another Australian study,
Little details personnel, public relations, consumer affairs and more
recently corporate social responsibility, as women's chosen fields.[2]
Gail Radford found a similar situation in the Australian Public Service,

646622

and referred to these areas as 'soft areas—women's work'[3]. It seems that women have been, consciously or unconsciously, choosing the 'velvet ghettos' as their work areas.[4] While legitimate choices, these areas are essentially staff functions and peripheral to the more established and powerful line functions of sales, finance and production. The latter are left to men who subsequently rise to occupy all the main management positions.

Women's preference for 'feminine' type occupations or sex-typed roles thus limits their career development because their chosen jobs and functions are marginal to an organisation's continued existence. 'Oh, that's not true', you might say. 'There is nothing more important than the personnel or training function in an organisation. In that role you are developing people for the future. How can that *not* be important?'

Well, who gets either fired or closed down when times become hard? Personnel, training and advertising! These are cost centres, not profit areas, and are therefore expendable when the 'bottom line' dictates action. Development is sacrificed to economics. It will pay you to remember this if you are bent on becoming a Human Resource Manager or Director!

It can be argued that women have few alternatives—that is, they are locked into these marginal areas because few organisations, or men, will allow them to function in any other. While there is some truth in this, it is pointless looking for scapegoats. Like it or not, women tend to prefer these areas. Building on what they have been taught are their natural talents, women drift towards these occupations—a drift which could hardly be turned around in one generation.

THE BOTTOM LINE

If you are in a predictable 'woman's' area, your current career choice may have one of these effects:

- You may become locked into this marginal area and have no career future. The longer you stay in that area, the harder it will be for you to move. After all, you may not have had any other experience which is of use to the organisation.

- Your functional selectivity (those 'interesting' jobs that you have chosen), will mean that you will rarely be selected for line management or other areas which contribute to profits (unless you are in a specialist marketing, advertising or public relations firm or consultancy). You are labelled as a 'specialist', one who cannot contribute to mainstream profitmaking.

■ You will also be overlooked when appointments to Boards, Statutory Authorities or Commissions are made because you do not have the 'qualifications and experience' for these roles. Unless you have had line management experience or understand the 'bottom line' it is doubtful that shareholders will trust their funds to your judgement because you have no credibility.

■ You will receive few career training and development opportunities because the role you occupy is not important to the organisation. Why develop you if you are not going anywhere? The *Women in Management Study* found few women were being given these opportunities in comparison to men because they were employed mainly in marginal areas. Organisations usually only invest money in employees who are earmarked for senior management. While a social conscience and recognition of disadvantaged groups may be very topical, money is rarely expended on 'peripherals' like training and development unless the organisation can be sure that the individual will return like for like by way of contribution to profits, products or strategic growth areas.

■ You may also suffer a considerable wage differential because you are in a non-mainstream career area. In case you disagree (particularly if you consider your own salary as high), look at the evidence provided in Table 5.1 on the comparative salary earnings of men and women managers from 239 Australian organisations. Notice how the salary ranges for men and women managers differ significantly nearer the top of the hierarchy. Some women are definitely being underpaid despite equal pay legislation and the rhetoric that accompanies it.

■ As times become harder you may be offered a career alternative, like job sharing or part-time work. Before you jump at this chance because it will give you time to do other things, remember that job sharers or part-time workers *never* reach senior management. You are falling into a trap, an age old one which Australian Census figures reveal has kept women at the bottom for most of their working careers. Your career will have been thwarted because you have not stopped to think of the implications of these 'new' social moves to improve conditions in the workplace.

If you disagree then you are not truly serious about a career. Ambitious achievers will recognise the danger signs quite clearly. You have to be always on the alert when you are competing for a career. You have to guard against not only your fellow competitors— your colleagues—but also the organisations for which you work. Everyone may have the best of intentions, but when you make a choice it creates a reaction. And that reaction can go against you if you are not careful!

Giving up? Of course not. Remember that the truly ambitious never give up just because they are faced with seemingly insurmountable hurdles. You have to know what the facts are, and how they pertain to your career prospects, before you can take remedial action. Just hoping for rescue is insufficient. These are the facts, unpleasant and unpalatable as they may be. Regretfully, not many women know

Table 5.1   Comparative Average Salary Levels for Men and Women in the Management Structure (1985)

Management Level	Men managers		Women managers
	Type A organisation (N = 101)	Type B organisation (N = 138)	
Average salary Supervisors	$22,627	$21,337	$19,875
Junior Managers	$25,933	$24,564	$23,111
Middle Managers	$33,189	$31,398	$28,391
Senior Managers	$46,890	$44,145	$35,542
Salary range Supervisors	$17,000– 38,000	$16,000– 40,000	$15,000– 25,000
Junior Managers	$19,000– 50,000	$20,000– 47,000	$18,000– 34,000
Middle Managers	$26,000– 63,000	$25,000– 62,000	$23,000– 60,000
Senior Managers	$30,000– 100,000	$32,000– 98,000	$30,000– 64,000

Note: 1   Type A organisations are firms with no women managers.
Type B organisations are firms with women managers.

2   Twenty-five (18%) of Type B organisations were unable to provide data for this section, compared to 12 per cent of Type A organisations.

them. They labour on believing they are making progress, which in many ways they are. But the progress could be greater if they knew the whole scenario. So lift your spirits and remember that many women have made it through the reefs when the odds were even greater. If they can, so can you. You are not alone.

AVOIDING THE PITFALLS

What should you do to avoid the pitfalls? The following advice may help.

When you secure a new job, examine the hierarchy. Are there many or few promotional steps? Do they involve line management roles or are they just more interesting but specialist roles? What sort of titles go with these jobs—manager, director or just officer? Do the jobs have status within the hierarchy?

If the answer is no, then work for a couple of years to get some qualifications and experience in a certain area and *move on.*

If the answer is yes, then you are in a position and organisation which appears to offer you a *career future.* The *Women in Management* study found that most women were promoted from *within* their organisations rather than being promoted from outside. There may be no need to look elsewhere if you choose wisely in the first instance.

Endeavour to avoid work areas which have large concentrations of women. No matter how much you may like the company of your own sex, and have a high regard for their ability and competence, it is a sad fact of life that identification with groups of women, especially in the workplace, does not help your career. Just think back to those days when very capable women office managers managed large teams of women. Who got promotion? Certainly not the woman office manager—she was far too valuable. She was always left in charge at that level because no man could handle either the level (it was an insult to his career aspirations) or the women (what did he do it they became emotional?) While times are changing slowly, there is still this tendency to pigeon-hole women in certain areas. If you wish to break this nexus, then you will have to go and work *where the men are!*

You should also attempt to broaden your horizons by becoming involved in outside organisations. Professional associations are the most relevant because membership often leads to contacts which sometimes end in job offers. However, instead of just joining to receive newsletters and other material, you should actually go to meetings and serve on committees. To prevent yourself from being fenced in you must *become highly visible*. Men have known this for years. Note how willing they are to stand for office, no matter how lowly the position. They also know that they have to serve an apprenticeship before being considered for higher things. Women are not aware of these vital issues and consequently stay in the background, doing all the paper work. If you wish to avoid the career pitfalls, try to get elected to high office but make sure you don't do all the work. That should be left to your subordinates, who will replace you in the job when you choose to move on.

As mentioned earlier, you should also have a career goal. Should you be lucky enough to reach your destination earlier than expected, simply set another career goal. Although this may sometimes take some time to think over, the important thing is to *keep on going*. Many people give up after reaching their initial destination. Others simply choose to lead an easier life, tired of all the problems that success can bring. The truly ambitious, however, are never content to sit still. They must be doing something, and going somewhere. Most career success depends on *persistence*. You must have this if you wish to avoid the pitfalls described above.

Finally, you can overcome the traps of the 'velvet ghettos' by career-switching. It is now quite fashionable to have two or three careers in one life-time. The days are gone when you had to work 40 years in the same career to gain the 'right' amount of experience to be considered a 'serious' contender for promotion. While career-switching may involve doing extra courses, or working in areas you have never considered, you will find that you will come closer to the mainstream of organisations and have a real chance of a career. Even if there is no immediate promotion, you will have gained extra experience in more suitable areas which will qualify you for promotion in the years ahead.

Being 'buried' in an unsuitable job does not mean the end of your career. Many successful people have started out on their career paths in very unsatifactory situations. The important thing is to realise what is happening to you and to *take action*. Success never came to the fainthearted. Becoming a top woman manager involves constant vigilance, persistence and consistency.

RIGHTING THE DIRECTION

Serious career aspirants watch over their career development like 'mother hens'. Shrewd enough to recognise that life is not as good as it could be, or 'how did she get ahead faster than I, especially when I used to beat her at school?', they instinctively know the right strategies to assist them if their careers go astray.

For instance, they seek career counselling. Not content to be in dead-end jobs, feeling frustrated by their working environment, they ask someone for help and advice. Usually this advice comes from men, since they know the ways of the working world, the rules of the game. Women are not as knowledgeable or experienced. The right career counselling has been known to 'mature' many a career.

The career-minded also look for 'acting' or apprenticeship positions, no matter how humble. They accept every opportunity to act while others are absent through either annual leave or illness, hoping that their superiors will notice their abilities and talents. Should things not work out as expected, they can always fall back on the excuse they they were just 'stand ins'. Their 'credit-worthiness' is unaffected as the position was not permanent. They never say, 'Oh! no! I couldn't! I just wouldn't know what to do!' They grasp the opportunity with both hands. Ambitious women should emulate this behaviour because such acting opportunities are particularly rare for women.

The career-minded also look for positions that have an apprenticeship element to them—at the 'foot of the master'. You never know where such positions will lead. Protégés have been know to inherit the mantles of the powerful following their retirement, promotion or transfer. Remember, however, that protégés are never too proud to do menial tasks, or put up with temperamental superiors. They keep their eyes on the long-term goal and are prepared to pay the short-term price.

When all else fails, serious career-seekers have been known to take sabbaticals. Borrowed from the academic stream, the term means 'time out' for reflection, reassessment, repose and righting the direction. Some career-seekers have been know to take several years off to 'do their own thing'—whatever that may be. They then re-enter the mainstream and become even more successful. The sabbatical has allowed them to re-orient their thinking and ambitions or just allowed time off for a well earned rest.

NIRVANA

What path should you take to senior management? Much will depend on your industry and occupation. However, one can say that the following are generally *avoided* by the upwardly-mobile:

- specialist roles (unless you are gaining qualifications or experience, but make sure the stay does not become permanent);

- jobs which are in staff or service areas, unless the whole firm is devoted to this functional purpose, such as a personnel consultancy;

- women's areas or ghettos, such as equal employment opportunity. While socially desirable, and correcting many past social inequities, these areas are considered to be peripheral, and a burden to mainstream organisational functioning (in case you disagree, reflect on the comments made about the 'cost' of implementing equal employment opportunity);

- positions which may be labelled management but in which no real managerial responsibility, such as managing people, is involved. These positions may have the salary of management, but everybody knows the position has no power or status in the organisation.

Nirvana comes from the following career tracks:

- line management—no matter what description. The usual rungs are junior, middle, senior management, and perhaps a seat on the Board;

- your own business—no matter what kind—where you can be managing director, chairman of the Board, or just a plain entrepreneur;

- non-traditional areas for women, such as finance, accountancy, futures markets, production and sales;

- the 'flavour of the month' occupations. Like everything else occupational fashions come and go. Sometimes industrial relations specialists reign paramount; sometimes it is marketing; other times it is the accountants; these days it seems to be high finance and currency dealers. Nirvana is the fashionable occupation. Read the papers and observe; the indicators are there. That's why career-switching is also in fashion. The ambitious are always ready for the long jump. Career-switching enables you to reposition yourself in what is currently mainstream. You are no longer locked out, but have re-oriented you career path to areas which have a future. You have shown your initiative and have earmarked yourself as among the 'new breed' of woman.

On which career track are you? Only you can decide which path you wish to follow. Only you can decide whether to accept this advice or ignore it.

POLISHING THE IMAGE

Ambitious women know that successful people do not reach the top in management unaided. Not only must they have a good career track record, they also have to know how to present themselves in the career environment. This does not mean the choice of clothes, hairdresser, suburb, office suite or limousine. It means knowing how to present at interviews, either for new jobs or promotion or the Board appointment.

Ambitious women have a 'bloodhound' component to their natures. Scenting career success in the wind, they make sure that they present the 'right' image. Consequently, they are particularly careful about how they go about their next career move. The following ground rules enable you to win the required 'brownie points'.

The opener: the CV

The career-minded forward to prospective employers a pristine white curriculum vitae, which has been prepared by means of a laser printer, an electronic typewriter or appropriate word processor. In case you do not have access to such facilities, less modern technological means of preparation are still considered acceptable, provided the finished product has a good format.

The trick is to make your cv stand out from those of other applicants. Shrewd people have been known to put theirs in unusual folders, and to use different coloured paper to highlight key points in a career. Others have even presented 'portfolios' of school reports, testimonials, photographs and other items. This is going a little too far, unless you want a job in Hollywood or the media. Most executives are still conservative and don't want to feel too threatened by a job applicant (remember most have earned their success by long apprenticeships, not by leap-frogging).

Good cvs are nicely typed, beautifully spaced (with highlighter headings at appropriate intervals), and give all the information needed to answer any questions in the interviewer's mind. They contain all necessary dates and details arranged in a rational order so that the reader does not have to hunt to see what you can do. (It is surprising how many people leave out important points in their cvs, while others include the most irrelevant details. Ask anyone involved in the employment of labour. You haven't completed your education until you observe what other people think is important!

A well presented and documented cv will usually get you on the short-list, provided the information you provide is *relevant to the job*. Some people send in cvs which are works of art. However, they also send the same information to all prospective employers—no matter what the job! They forget to alter the copy to suit the situation.

Others offend by attaching dog-eared photostat copies of career details to their application letter. In these days of word processors such a practice is unforgivable. It indicates that the applicant is unprepared to make the effort to create an impression. The employer is left with the idea (usually deliberate) that the applicant is applying for many jobs. However, instead of offering for the individual's services, the prospective employer is unimpressed.

The interview, or communicating with style

Being nicely dressed and arriving well in time for the interview is no longer sufficient in these times of shrinking job markets. Short-listed managerial applicants are now expected to make *presentations* on their strengths, weaknesses and potential contributions. Marketing yourself has become the name of the game. You, and your experience and background, are now a product. As a career-minded individual, you have to sell yourself to potential buyers. Simply answering questions in a bright and earnest fashion is not good enough. You have to present your 'wares' like a retailer. Packaging, display, logistics, and promotion are your secret weapons in the race to senior management. Mastery of these merchandising elements will give you confidence, style and flair. You will be earmarked as a winner, one who is destined for recognition and success.

Appalled by such news? This is not you. People are surely not conned by such confidence tricks? Prospective employers are looking for people who are going to work hard, fit in, and know how to be 'nice'. You will just go along to an interview and answer the questions truthfully. If you 'deserve' the job you will get it. Your record will speak for itself. You don't have to sell yourself like a packet of soap powder.

If this is what you think, be prepared to be left behind at the starting line. You have just made the most critical mistake of your life. When times become tough, and good jobs are few and far between (the history of womankind), it is no holds barred! The ambitious look around for ways and means to make themselves stand out from the pack. Women certainly do that because they are women. However, as most lack the critical skills, qualifications and experience to win the final race against stronger competitors, adopting such attitudes merely rules you out before the race has even begun.

Like it or not, managerial job applicants are mastering the rules of presentation for their next career move. Some even *rehearse* their answers to potential questions before being interviewed in order to exhibit a smooth confident style. Not for them the 'ums' and 'ers' while they frantically search for an answer. Their friends help them simulate the interview in order to be able to deal with the unexpected. They wish to give the impression of being on top of things. Experienced job applicants know that interviewers usually ask fairly standard questions. If you are unaware of these, then apply for some jobs and be interviewed. Experience is the greatest teacher.

Carolyn, 37, and a personnel consultant, reports:

> I never cease to be amazed by the number of managers who don't know how to apply for a job. That applies to the way they present their information in the first place, and how they come across at interview. Most are intelligent individuals, but they have no idea of how to go about creating an impression so that someone would actually want to employ them. They just sit there and expect others to recognise their good qualities and their hidden potentiality immediately. I guess it is an ego thing, but it makes this job very difficult at times.
>
> For instance, we were recently interviewing for a fairly important job. Our client was looking for an 'up-and-comer'—a 'go-getter'. However, the people whom we interviewed turned out to be a mixed bag. Some of the men looked good on paper, with all the right qualifications and experience, but presented very poorly. With one man I almost had to drag his answers out of him. He may have been nervous but we were offering very high money. The client would not be interested in someone who became tongue-tied under stress.
>
> Others presented a very laid-back style. In fact some didn't even bother to put a tie on—times are changing, even in business! They left you with the impression they were doing you a favour in just turning up for the interview.
>
> I'm used to that from men applicants. But it was the women applicants who really interested me. Their cvs were difficult to read (one rambled on for about 30 pages); they didn't have sufficient experience for the job but were almost demanding that they be

appointed because of EEO, while many couldn't even articulate what their contribution would be to the organisation. Most just said that they had 'expertise' (actually unproven) and that they should be given a chance to do the job. Perhaps. But they will have to come up with better reasons than that.

Unfortunately, the client would not be impressed with such a recommendation. I think women have a lot to learn now that they are trying to establish careers. The first skill they should acquire is how to sell themselves at interviews—that is, talk in terms of contributions, skills and abilities—rather than repeat the rhetoric of the EEO movement.

Harsh words? Maybe. Remember they come from a woman who knows women aspirants at first hand. While she is sympathetic to women and their problems, her common sense also ensures that she serves the client's best interests. If women do not make the grade, no matter how disadvantaged they have been in the past, they are not recommended for positions.

Reconsidering the marketing issue? If you can overcome your natural aversion, try and use some of these tactics next time you apply for a management position:

- Before submitting an application, contact the organisation for information. Such calls often tell you whether or not you should apply, because you will have elicited details of the job, the people with whom you will be working and the organisation's products and services. Don't ask, 'Is it worth my while to apply?' Only you can decide that. Such questions raise two issues in the receiver's mind: you are not interested in taking the trouble to make an application unless you are going to be successful (and who can tell? This will usually depend on the interview and the other competitors); and you want a guarantee that you will get the job over other applicants (sight unseen).

- Research the organisation. After all, annual reports, stock exchange information and other organisational literature are easily obtainable. Just ring up and inquire. Talk to people in the industry to get the competitor's viewpoint of the organisation and its people. Talk to actual employees. The more information you can obtain the more prepared you are. You can tailor your application to suit the needs; and you will be better equipped at the interview stage.

- Rehearse your answers to possible questions if short-listed for interview. Either write out your answers and memorise them, or have a friend play question and answer. Rehearsal or practice will prepare you for those unexpected 'curly' moments which occur at all interviews. If this sounds degrading, remember that interviewing, like acting, is an art and needs to be practised for skill to be acquired.

■ Work out your strengths, weaknesses and possible contributions before the interview. If you can't analyse yourself, get someone to do it professionally or ask your friends. The trick is to maximise your strengths and to minimise your lesser points. Remember the golden rule: emphasise the positive. Don't mention your weaknesses, but if questioned about them admit them and then move on to why they should be ignored or can be minimised (your strengths are so overwhelming). The organisation must feel that it would suffer a great loss if you did not join the team.

■ Don't be aggressive about how good you are because modesty is still considered a virtue. Bluster, aggression, or being 'hale and hearty' does not fit too well with the cultivated image of the successful woman. The skill is to appear confident rather than aggressive (which will have been helped by the prior rehearsals). Questions should be answered in a direct, forthright and succinct manner—no rambling or clutching your throat with your hand! In fact, bury your hands. Interviewers always look for trembling fingers. Successful people know these points and don't draw attention to the obvious fact that they are nervous.

■ Should the questions not reveal you to best advantage, take charge. This doesn't mean swapping seats with the interviewer— just take charge of your answers! Borrow a favourite technique of the clever media interviewee: no matter what question is asked, give the answer you want to give. If you have been unable to sell yourself, or your contribution, then try and ensure that you do in your answers to the remaining questions. If asked only a few questions, sum up with a presentation of your key points (to tell the interviewer why you should get the job). Remember that you are being evaluated in terms of others. If interviewers can't evaluate you, then do it for them. You provide the convincing arguments on why they should employ you—not them!

■ Remain cool, calm and collected when faced with interviewing panels. Top job applicants are usually scrutinised this way. Consensus decision-making is now the order of the day. Judgements are made by teams, not individuals. Under such circumstances, prior rehearsal of presentations becomes even more important. You may have to impress up to ten people who are looking for the slightest flaw. Don't flinch or waver. Women applicants perform extremely well in these situations. Men are much more nervous and have sometimes been known to faint!

- Above all, emphasise your potential contribution. Ignore sexist remarks or questions, and impolite suggestions. Top women candidates also do not discuss child care arrangements, flexitime, days off for shopping, holidays to coincide with school vacations, or the social club. Concentrate on what you can offer the organisation.

Marketing yourself can actually be fun. Once involved you begin to look for ways to improve your performance. Women have a natural flair for this. So overcome your aversions. You have no better product to sell than yourself. Remember that managers, either male or female, are expected to be confident and marketing is one of the tools of trade. A marketing affinity has helped many a stalled career make its way to the top. Ignore marketing yourself at your peril. The best jobs go to the best promoters, and not everyone can afford an advertising agency or personal publicist.

OUTCOMES AND OPTIONS

While marketing skills help you to get more offers, acceptances, rejections and bargaining positions also require panache, just like interviews. Men have been known to 'think things over' while they consider other offers. Women are not so fortunate. They either have to accept the job or not (after all, 'who else would employ a mere woman? This organisation is going out on a limb in just offering her the position'). Don't take too long to make up your mind. Manager's are supposed to know their own minds. Accept any reasonable offer graciously, quickly and without fuss—and as long as it suits your career purposes. Your new employers will continue to be impressed with your professional approach.

Should the offer not suit you, then decline just as graciously. Avoid arguments about how 'sexist' they are. The employer will be relieved —and even more impressed with your professional approach!

Alternatively, if bargaining and negotiating are the order of the day, keep calm, be objective. Many an advantage has been lost by too hasty an acceptance or rejection. Get some tips on strategies from experts, or observe others bargaining. Keep to simple rules. You have an advantage. Men, and organisations, do not expect women to be able to negotiate to win.

Finally, if all else fails, seek advice on why you were unsuccessful. Organisations will often give you this information once they get over their embarrassment. While the same circumstances will not apply the next time around, you may discover some unknown weaknesses. That information is worth the price of failure, because you will have the chance to deal with the weakness—or camouflage it at the next interview!

THE ROAD TO SUCCESS

You know you are on the road to success when you are sought out by a 'headhunter'. Skilled in ferreting out the 'up and comers' through recommendation and performance, the professional headhunter will never let you go once you are in his or her sights. Be patient. While nothing may come from the initial sallies (the first arranged interviews), you are gaining visibility and exposure to other opportunities. Eventually you will be placed, and usually in positions which you may not have been able to obtain yourself. Remember that the best jobs are never advertised—they are let out for placement to professional 'executive search' firms. The headhunter's call means that your reputation is growing and you are making an impact. But remember you still have to perform in your new job despite being searched out for placement. The grapevine will carry your failures more rapidly than your successes.

Furthermore, don't boast about being headhunted. While this may be exciting, discretion is always the better part of valour. Headhunters don't like their activities becoming public property. They are hired because they are discreet and reputable—not because they broadcast their 'catches' like fishing contests. Should the new career move not work out, you want to be considered worthy of replacement in the years ahead. Top career people are discreet because the stakes are very high. You want to keep moving to your destination as a top woman manager, and not be sidetracked down a branch line.

ASKING FOR MORE MONEY

Top achievers never discuss money. This is usually left to lawyers, negotiating teams, business managers, professional agents—and immediate family. Most of us are not yet at that stage. What do you do, then, to earn a raise?

As previously revealed, women are not in the same monetary stakes as their male counterparts. However, while this is the last taboo in terms of equality, we are still entitled to a fair distribution. How to achieve this? Consider the following:

- You can earn more money by making a career move—usually to another job in another organisation. Women often have to job-hop to be paid their due. However, you may be considered uncommitted and unreliable because you don't hold a job for any length of time.

- You can ask your present employer for more, and you may receive it. Alternatively you may be offered something else, like a company car, an entertainment allowance, or a trip overseas. Hard cold cash may be difficult to come by (consider the taxation), but at least you will be ahead of your earlier situation.

- 'High flyers' (those the organisation can't really do without) may actually negotiate a share of profits, revenue, or any other measuring stick. You are now in a situation where you could even become rich! However, you could just as equally lose if the firm goes bust. You will also have be confident that you can increase profits because your income will depend on continued growth.

- Again, you can do a survey of similar positions and see where you stand in relation to the mid-point. Providing the information to your employer may help towards a decision in your favour.

- Obtaining another position can also have the same effect, provided you are wanted by your current employer. There is nothing so effective as another bidder to suddenly elicit a rise, even in stringent economic times. However, resignation is not a good idea. You may overplay your hand and find that you are no longer even in management!

These are all tried and trusted strategies, but women, it seems, don't like to ask ('What ever will they think of me?'). You must overcome this reticence and be more forthright. Then you will receive one of two things: a raise in salary or an invitation to leave the firm. At least you will know where you stand. Why linger where you are not really wanted? That information will save you time as you continue your progress.

ASKING FOR PROMOTION

The promotional hurdle is another difficult one for women. Just as money can be hard to ask for, so are promotions—even when deserved. Most women expect that their efforts and performance will be recognised. Regretfully, you will usually have to point out your case to others. In fact, in some cases you may even have to 'jump up and down' to receive your just rewards. If necessary, do it. Otherwise you will not be rewarded. Remember that women are usually *invisible* in management, especially when it comes to promotion. How to overcome invisibility?

- Inundate your superiors with copies of your memos and reports (But make sure that what you say is important and relevant).

- Tell people about your successes, how you are responsible for such and such a report, or such and such a project. If no one disagrees with you, your reputation will be helped. Promotions usually go to those who initiate something important.

- Make sure that you get invitations to all the important business and social events. Mix with people; be seen by everyone. A high profile usually brings recognition.

- Accept all invitations to speak and appear. As you become known, you can lessen the tempo (and have a rest).

- Finally, suggest a new job in the organisation which only you can perform. Make sure you spell out the contribution to the company, and have your successor already trained. Ensure that the new job is higher up the management ladder, and more visible than your last role.

Now that you know the secrets there is no reason for you to stray. Career achievers stay on the main track: they do not divert onto side lines.

One final word: when things get difficult (as they surely will), don't lose your conviction. Begin to waver, or have second thoughts, or listen to someone else (those 'kind' people who always have your best interests at heart) and your momentum will diminish.

If you have made an incorrect decision, change your direction. The effects of a bad decision remain with you until you make a new decision. At all times, keep going. As Helen Keller said, 'You may not end up where you originally intended, but you will achieve a considerably higher position and sometimes in a whole new direction'. When you can answer 'Where are you going?' you are on the main trunk route: the pathway to senior management.

6

Piggybacking up the hierarchy

ONE OF THE most valuable things you can learn in your climb to senior management is 'how to win friends and influence people'. These friends are like 'assets', or money in the bank, to be drawn upon when the need arises. In case you feel squeamish about the use of friends in this way, remember two things: it is an accepted part of managerial life, and everyone else is doing it to you. Successful managers learn to have two types of 'friends'. The first are your real friends—those you have usually had since childhood or for a long time and who will stand by you at all times. The second are acquaintances and contacts made during the course of your career and who may desert you any time, even when you most need them.

The friends that most managers have to 'massage' during their managerial career fall into the latter group. These contacts are normally only 'user friendly' while you are 'user friendly'. Fall from grace, fail to return a favour or meet an obligation, and you will be deserted by them. It pays to understand these basic rules.

Successful managers adopt winning friends and influencing people as one of their key career strategies. Management mythology abounds with tips on how to implement the strategy and 'succeed in business without really trying'. Hollywood has enshrined images of neophytes who have learned to 'oil their way across the floor'. Men managers often use the strategy as the quickest way to 'piggyback' up the hierarchy. Women are novices in this, although they are now being presented with a number of avenues to enable them to play the game.

SISTERHOOD

Perhaps the most interesting of these has been the rise of the 'sisterhood'. The female version of 'mateship', it introduces women to other women and provides support, encouragement and counsel to those who feel beleaguered by the male managerial world. For perhaps the first time, women are both 'looking out' for other women and promoting them, recognising the truth of the old saying, 'United we stand, divided we fall'!

Sisterhood will do the following for you:

- It introduces you to powerful women who may use their own contacts to smooth your career path. Many prominent women are now asked by organisations to recommend other women for nomination to Boards and other important committees.

- It provides successful female role models as an alternative to the masculine managerial model. Numerous options are available: women who head their own businesses to women who are senior executives in large organisations. The choice is yours. Select your own role model and you will find numerous examples to follow.

- The role models also understand their obligations to the sisterhood. Having successfully achieved, and knowing the pitfalls of the climb, they are prepared to give help and guidance to similarly minded women. Where the climb may have been long in their own case, they are prepared to shorten it for the next generation. The aim is to provide chances to get more women into management.

- Sisterhood is also establishing its own mythology about women in management. By providing a history of others' experience, it allows aspiring achievers to feel less insecure and alone. It is comforting to learn that others have faced the same situations as you and *won*. Sisterhood thus provides continuing encouragement.

Of course, sisterhood also has its negative aspects. Consider the following:

- The 'founding mothers' of some groups have been known to want to keep control of both members and activities. Having initiated the group for sisterhood purposes, they become 'gatekeepers' of the group's integrity, morals, philosophy and purpose. Control remains firmly in their hands no matter how many women come within the group's ambit. While there is little wrong with this in theory, the restrictions in practice exclude many women for not meeting the 'criteria'. Sisterhood can thus be as exploitative and restrictive to women as 'mateship' has been in the past.

- Sisterhood also has its own 'cliques and gangs'. Be excluded from the inner circle or decision-making group, and you will rarely find out what's going on. The inner circle gets the jobs, the publicity, the favours, the perks—no matter what the qualifications and experience of its members. They receive the bounty and special consideration because they are part of the inner group, another female version of a despised male tactic.

- Sisterhood also has its own form of 'mafia' to teach other women who has the power when they offend the sensitivities of those in control. Imagined slights are dealt with in the same way as real injustices. The offender is singled out by the network system within the sisterhood. She is soon aware of her transgression because her 'contacts' begin to avoid her.

In case you think this last statement is a little strong, the following two incidents illustrate what can happen to women who find themselves on the wrong side of sisterhood wrath. Both incidents were over 'interpretable' matters. However, the results were devastating to the women concerned as the sisterhood took its revenge.

Robyn relates her story:

I first became aware that all was not well with my friends when I went to a women's luncheon and was positively ignored by many of the women whom I knew quite well. I felt very uneasy until one of the women, whom I had previously considered an ally and helper, came up to me gushingly and asked how the sales of my first book were going (I had just written a book on women). Before she left I asked her why another friend had refused to review the book for a women's magazine. She replied that I was not in favour—in fact, the woman reviewer was very annoyed with me—because I had made some slighting remarks in the book about a group we were all members of and its activities.

I was stunned because what she was saying was completely untrue. I had not even mentioned this group she was referring to, so couldn't understand why I was 'out of favour'. What did alarm me, however, was that a group of women whom I had previously believed were quite supportive towards me were now acting as a censorship group and denying the book access to publicity. I told her that I was very surprised at this action and she just offhandly said, 'If you don't like it go and see the editor of the magazine: she's over there'.

I immediately made representations to the editor who was very embarrassed to be caught in the middle of a private dispute. However, she did promise to look into the matter for me and a few days later rang me to say that the book had not been reviewed (it had been returned with no explanation) and that she would arrange another review for publication. I at least felt vindicated, especially when my own re-reading of the book failed to reveal where I had slighted this particular women's group and its activities.

I waited several months for the review to appear. It didn't. What did eventuate was a mere mention of the book on one of the pages of the magazine. Hardly the type of review I was expecting!

In the meantime I also became aware that my publisher was having difficulty in getting the book reviewed by the women's pages in the newspapers. Where there was great excitement initially, and promises of edited versions, the book was returned unreviewed. I suddenly twigged to what was going on. All these women knew each other—that is, the woman who first refused to review the book and the women who controlled the women's pages. A conspiracy was operating! The censorship had now spread from one reviewer to cut off many avenues of promotion. I was being 'done in' by a female 'mafia' and there was no way they were going to let my book receive the attention it deserved.

Needless to say, the book did sell. Other women's groups took it up and promoted it heavily. It also made the newspapers—but in different columns to those controlled by this female group. It has been a valuable lesson to me. I have learnt the power of the sisterhood, but have also realised that you can still succeed without it.

The whole incident was over something entirely different and personal. What the woman really took offense at was that she was not included in the book (I had interviewed her as part of my research). She didn't know that she was to be included in another book. If she had spoken to me, rather than taking her unilateral and biased action, all would have been explained. Her revenge tactics were completely unnecessary!

Women formerly escaped such unpleasant and revengeful incidents, mainly because there were so few of them and they were not in positions of power. However, times have changed and women can now exert considerable influence on other women's careers, aspirations and even earning potential (for example, the sales of the book). Robyn's story reveals how powerful that influence can be.

Martha's story is perhaps even more disturbing, because it reveals an even worse aspect of the sisterhood: the tendency of some members to exert a form of intellectual suppression!

I had just joined this new women's group and was pleased to be able to have contact with like-minded women from time to time. However, I became somewhat worried when the group began to discuss potential members (membership was by invitation only). Various names were suggested, and their qualifications for membership discussed. Suddenly one member said that she wouldn't be interested in a certain Ms X joining because she had never done anything for women!

This was somewhat of a surprise because the particular woman under discussion was very prominent, and had been a pioneer for women in many fields. It then transpired that many of the other women held the same opinion about her. She had offended them because at one time she had been quoted as saying that women should work for a career; that they weren't dedicated enough and should serve an apprenticeship—that is, go on committees and earn their success—rather than expect it to be handed to them on a platter.

I was very disturbed by my colleagues' response to this woman. While they may not have agreed with her opinions this was no reason to exclude her from the group. Their action was also revealing something about them: unless you thought as they did, they were prepared to impose a form of intellectual suppression. No contrary views would be tolerated! I blurted this out: and everyone sat there silent.

It wasn't just women's normal bitchiness: this was a serious attempt to impugn another woman's standing and reputation in the community. Where had all the supportive women gone? This woman had actually done a lot for other women—much more than those who were now judging her—and she was an excellent role model. I was offended by what they were trying to do.

Later the woman who raised the initial objection withdrew it but the damage was done. Ms X was not invited to join, and I have been to only one meeting of the group since that time. I suspect they will probably be applying the 'thought criteria' to me in my absence. Talk about *1984*! It is well and truly alive in the women's movement! Women will never advance if this is how they behave when they get together.

Overreaction? Perhaps. But Robyn's story was another form of the same thing: intellectual suppression and censorship because the opinions of certain women did not coincide with those who held control. Women used to complain about being locked out of men's groups for the same reason. What they used to despise some are now practising themselves within their own organisational units.

Unpleasant as these two stories are, they illustrate what can happen. These are rare occurrences and the sisterhood is usually extremely supportive. However, as competition for the senior jobs becomes fiercer, such incidents are likely to become more common. Women are now competing against other women—not just men. It is as well you remember this.

NETWORKING

Networking is currently being promoted as a panacea for all of a managerial woman's ills. Should you feel lost, lonely or just plain unknowledgeable about something, then networking will provide support, succour and perhaps even information. On a more serious note, networking, like the sisterhood, is a means of winning friends and influencing people. Do a favour, and be done a favour in return. Reciprocity is the keynote.

Some people have a more pragmatic approach to networking. For instance, Harragan considers the only purpose of a network is '. . . constant, cold-blooded discussion and analysis of what jobs are worth in a competitive male market and how much your services are worth in comparison. . .'[1]

However, Australian women have yet to reach such levels of sophistication. The majority does not realise that this is the prime purpose of networking. Most still want to get to know other people for their own sakes, rather than consider how they can help them up the ladder to success. There is a reflected glory from mixing with people who have achieved. It also helps a woman's self-esteem to be included in a special group. At present, then, networking is really an extension of the sisterhood movement. Women are still feeling their way along this new avenue.

Nevertheless, the networking process is slowly spreading among aspiring women. Originating in many professional organisations as a means around the 'invisible woman' barrier, networking is now incorporated into the practices of specific-interest women's groups and loose associations of women in particular levels of management and the professions. The 'elite' women have their own forms of networks, both formalised and unformalised, which are a far cry from afternoon teas, charity drives or Black and White Balls. These 'top drawer' networks are more like the version mentioned by Harragan. By invitation only, they comprise a limited number of top women in various sectors of the economy. Their networking practices operate at two levels: to get to know similar like-minded women who may be able to supply information or resources; and to fraternise with top men—either managing directors or entrepreneurs—for similar purposes. The latter arrangement may also be a source of mentors, guides, sponsors and career counselling. Given time these 'top drawer' women's networks could easily develop into a female version of the exclusive male Committee for Economic Development in Australia (CEDA) group and the Business Council of Australia (BCA).

Who benefits from networking? Alison Baines feels it is the following:

- women returning to work: networking allows them entry to the women's movement and also provides them with information and a chance to 'catch up';
- women just starting out in a career, particularly in competitive situations where contact with other women and other women's contacts may help them to achieve;
- women who work in isolation, either in male-dominated areas, or more often as 'loners'—that is, as consultants, part-timers or freelancers;
- politically aware women who feel strongly about a particular issue or who want to catalyse social change. Networking gives them access to like-minded individuals and establishes a power base;
- already 'established' women who just want to know other women at a similar level or to help younger women.[2]

However, women need to expand their horizons a little more. For instance, a recent Australian study[3] compared how 137 men and 115 women managers networked. Women used some features of the networking process quite well, others not so well. Consider how women varied from men in the practice of networking:

- Seeking new employment: men consulted men (usually a superior or colleague), while women consulted just about everybody—men and women, superiors and non-superiors, family and colleagues (possibly because it was harder for them to find good jobs).
- Helping others to find new employment: men helped men (usually a superior or colleague); women helped other men, and then women.
- Promotional advice and financial assistance: men consulted men (usually colleagues and professional contacts). For career counselling, women consulted women colleagues and professional contacts, and friends of both genders. For financial assistance, they consulted family and relatives.
- Professional associations/groups: men used these for business contacts, educational reasons, financial advice, and to promote their own business or company. They also held executive or leadership positions on committees. Women were more active in the groups (that is, in attending meetings), but mainly went for social and educational reasons. Few held executive roles on committees or used the group for promotion of their own business or company. Moreover, men were more involved than women in helping other members of these associations. People consulted men to help them gain new employment, to give financial advice, to help promote another's business and to be a business contact. Women executives were approached mainly as professional contacts who may be of assistance at a later stage.
- Social networking interactions: men entertained other male business/professional contacts for lunch, while women associated with other women business/professional/social contacts.
- For after-hours activities—a drink or dinner—men preferred other male business and professional contacts; women associated with other female business/professional/social contacts, and mixed gender groups.
- Venues chosen by the men for entertaining were clubs, restaurants and outdoor venues such as yachts and cruisers. Women preferred restaurants and the home.
- Weekend contacts: family and sporting contacts were more

important to the men that the women. While both had a similar amount of contact with community-related friends, women had more contacts with business/professional contacts at weekends than men (probably because many women executives were single).

■ Community-related organisations: men favoured service, political, sporting and recreation-type organisations which have a high profile in the male managerial culture for networking purposes. Women favoured socio-cultural and feminist-type organisations which have a low profile.

The study revealed that Australian women still have a lot to learn about networking, especially in the social arena. They tend to want to mix with friends while men are much more pragmatic. Their motto seems to be 'why waste time?' If entertaining has to be done, then let it be for business. In that way you kill two birds with one stone— relaxation and business. Women still need to have friends around them, to talk to and relax. Men have their eye only on the goal—a lesson the ambitious woman needs to learn.

If you are wondering how you can break into networks, the answer is simple. Join a few women's organisations like the Australian Federation of Business and Professional Women (BPW), and Women And Management (WAM)—called WIM in Victoria. Both have 'networking' sessions at the ends of meetings. Other professional women's groups are also adopting this practice. Alternatively, become either very 'visible' in the media or 'notorious' for something to do with women's issues and you will soon find yourself inundated with invitations to join various exclusive groups. You will be on your way, with an invisible web of contacts to help you. One thing you should remember about networks: don't remain exclusively in the female domain, no matter how supportive and comforting that may be. Men still make most of the decisions, so it will pay to move in some of their circles. Contact with men's groups and men's networks—even in the peripheral sense (they are after all still all-male domains despite EEO and social change)—may prove to be of more benefit to you in the longer term than involvement in the women's enclaves. A wise woman mixes in both circles, thereby increasing her chances for success.

SPONSORS AND MENTORS

Experience has shown that the fastest way to success is to be 'helped' along the way. Mentors and sponsors were the 'flavour of the month' until the controversy over the Cunningham/William Agee case. Since then, the concept has gone underground, to be talked of only to your intimates and researchers. It no longer pays to openly advertise that you have powerful friends. Networks and the sisterhood are more acceptable ways to camouflage support systems. And further admission is tantamount to career suicide!

Nevertheless, powerful sponsors or mentors have helped many a career to flourish. While not exactly in favour, the advantages of such an arrangement should not be underestimated.

Fiona gives an example from her career path:

Early on in my management career I was very fortunate to have a mentor/sponsor. I didn't realise what he was until years afterwards. That may seem strange, but I was in management long before the current crop of women. People just didn't talk about those concepts then.

This particular man was the most powerful man in the company—next to the family that controlled it. When I joined the organisation I didn't at first report to him, but after a management purge I suddenly found that he had 'taken me over'. I was petrified at first—used to go to his office in fear and trembling—because he had such a fearsome reputation. All my male colleagues went pale when he rang for them. He was just so ruthless, a man who had little education, but who had risen up the ranks the hard way.

My staff were quite pleased that I was reporting to him because, as they explained it to me, I would be able to get a decision and resources if my submissions pleased him. Under my former boss there was only delay, confusion and frustration.

The change in our relationship occurred one day after a rather strenuous meeting with a group of executives. As I was leaving he called me back and said, 'You had a win today'. I didn't quite know what he meant, but felt pleased. My second-in-charge, who had worked with him for many years, told me that I had persuaded him with my arguments and that was his way of letting me know.

Not long after that I was called up to his office for a talk. It was to be the first of many talks and many hours spent discussing a whole range of topics. Again, I didn't quite understand it because both of us were very busy. Then it dawned on me: I was giving him an education (I had several University degrees) and he was teaching me about management—his version.

As time went by our mutual respect for each other grew. He was a man I didn't like personally, but he had a fine brain and had some very strong principles (despite his reputation for ruthlessness). He was extremely fair in his dealings with others. It was his manner that put them off. He used to get so exasperated with all the lies, tales of woe and sheer inefficiencies of some of the people who worked for him. Of course, all my male colleagues thought I was having an affair with him and used to burst into his office from time to time to try and catch us in an embarrassing moment. All they ever saw was him on one side of the desk and me on the other. He also never called me by my first name. It was always Miss So and So, both in public and private. I did the same with him. I always called him Mr . . ., even when talking about him to my staff.

I developed very much as a manager under his guidance. It wasn't so much what he told me to do—it was rather that I would give the theoretical side of a management problem and he would speak from experience. I usually found that his version was correct. He really understood people and what they wanted.

Eventually he became Managing Director and I was also promoted to senior ranks—but not reporting to him. However, he still called me in for our talks, and always found ways of ensuring that I was working on one of his projects. He used to say that I was underutilised and needed to be kept busy. All he wanted was someone whom he could trust to do the job.

I left the company shortly before he retired. There just wasn't anyone else I wanted to work for. However, his lessons still stay with me today and I often think of how he might have done something when I have a management problem.

Fiona's case is unusual because her mentor didn't really help her career in the accepted sense—that is, by promotion. Instead he gave her an education in how to be an effective manager. He had an enormous impact on her life, and she has since found it difficult to work for others who do not measure up to his standards. In this sense she was both fortunate and unfortunate to have had the experience of working for an exceptional man. She also knew instinctively how far she could go with him. When it became obvious that she had his ear, everybody tried to have her make submissions on their behalf. She always refused because she knew that he would then have nothing to do with her. He was against people taking advantage of a situation, and Fiona herself always had to present a well argued case, backed up by copious figures, to win her points. Nothing was ever granted just because of their talks together.

Mentors normally provide guidance, career counselling and even help in obtaining promotions if you are lucky enough to strike the right individual. Sometimes there will be a well-established relationship between two people, as in Fiona's case. In other situations there will be a number of mentors. Help may be given randomly by many individuals as you pursue your career.

Such was the experience of Jennifer, aged 42. Now nearly at the top of her professional hierarchy, with only one more promotion to obtain before reaching the most senior position, she has received advice from time to time from a range of people. One was a schoolteacher who casually suggested she do a certain subject at school. This changed the direction of her whole life. Another was a speech therapist (Jennifer had a stutter), who suggested that she could face her problem by entering an occupation where talking was essential. And the other was a landlady who suggested that she try for anything that was going in terms of jobs. That gave her the confidence to apply for positions she would have otherwise been hesitant about. All three people played a minor role in her life, yet all three have had far-reaching influences.

Mentors, therefore, come in many forms. Some have been mothers or fathers; other have been lovers or husbands; more likely they have been bosses or colleagues in the working environment. Occasionally they have been religious advisors, schoolteachers, friends, or neighbours. It doesn't matter who they are. It is the help and guidance they give that is important. Men have long used the mentoring and sponsorship system to advantage. The business world usually knows who is the protege of whom. Wise women will observe and learn.

In case you feel that you have been neglected in this area, just remember that mentors and sponsors often seem to materialise as you become more visible and successful. Headhunters have also been known to fulfil that role. Get on the 'books' of an executive search firm and you may never have need of another sponsor—your career will be taken care of, providing you do the work! Successful people, or those with promise, usually attract advice and help.

One final point: always acknowledge a mentor or sponsor. No-one ever reaches senior management entirely on their own. It pays to remember who has helped you, even if it has been only a minor influence, in case you need these people again on the way down!

THE 'TAG' METHOD

The above three methods of 'piggybacking' up the hierarchy are generally acceptable. The tag method is *not*. It usually means riding on the coat-tails of someone else who is either gullible, stupid or just plain too busy to notice your scheming strategies. While you may have manoeuvred your way into the good graces of an achiever, everyone else knows your real plan—to gain promotion without doing any of the hard work yourself.

If the method is not acceptable, then, why give it space? Because, unfortunately, many people use the technique—some successfully. It is common in both scientific and academic circles where groups of people work together, researching and writing certain projects. It is becoming more common in management as the 'team' takes precedence over individual achievers. While everyone in the group may know who has done the hard work, others hear only the bragging of the one claiming the credit.

Women have long suffered not being given due credit. Schooled for years as secretaries, assistants, clerks, and general factotems, they have stood in the shadows when praise was being given. Often they have done all the work (it is called delegation by those in power) only to see someone else reap the reward. No voices were raised in protest, because a woman always knew her place—until now. Now that women are in the workforce, and are even in management, it is important that they be given due credit because a whole career can be built or falter on a false impression.

Witness the reaction of Kath, who found her ideas taken over by someone unworthy:

> I had just been appointed to this department and was quite honoured when the boss invited me to lunch. Over the entree he asked me if I have any ideas for the department—things I would like to try out. Foolishly, and glibly, I spent the next two hours telling him all my ideas about the job, the department and the company. Imagine my chagrin two days later when at a departmental meeting these same ideas were trotted out to the group as, 'I've been thinking about the direction we ought to go and these are my ideas'. Word for word! No changes at all! Except they were now *his* ideas and not mine! The worst of it was that I just sat there letting him do it. I was so new that I thought I couldn't speak against the boss and say: 'Wait—those are my ideas—you haven't given me any credit'. It really upset me. But what was worse I had let myself down. I didn't fight for my own ideas. I just let someone else take them and claim the credit. What I couldn't understand was how he could do it in front of me. It just seemed I didn't exist—I was the 'invisible woman' and he had just absorbed my ideas as his own.

Of course Kath's story was not an unusual one in that department. The boss did the same thing to all new staff—mainly because he had no ideas of his own and no progress was made until a new person was appointed. Unfortunately, his superiors knew nothing of his tactics and considered him to be innovative and dynamic, because every so often a tremendous idea was generated in the department.

If you wish to use the tag method you will have to adopt these tactics:

- Seek out all the young achievers in the organisation. Make sure they are fairly enthusiastic, hard workers and a little 'starry-eyed'. Offer to be a help-mate, to be part of the team, because you are 'in the know' about either the company, the boss, the Board, the customers, the environment—anything! However, make sure you don't do much work. Just put in an appearance at strategic meetings, say a few words, but always have to leave early for other more important matters. Because you have contributed at the beginning, people will feel obligated to include your name on the report. Be sure to tell everyone that it was your idea, and your work, when discussing the project. No-one is going to contradict you when they were not involved. But make sure the others are not in earshot—they may actually speak up when they get over their surprise!

- Alternatively, pick on some clever but socially deficient person in the organisation, someone with the potential for success but requiring help to smooth the way. Such people have all the ability but have never learned to play the political game. Once again offer to help them, to smooth the way. They will be so grateful for your assistance that they will even allow you to do the negotiating and presenting for them with top management. Of course, their unpolished manner and lack of social skills will necessitate their exclusion from the meeting. If the report proves to be successful, you will get the credit. If it proves otherwise you can always disassociate yourself from both the group and the project. You were merely representing them for the good of the company!

Another favourite ploy is to have your name first on any presentation material when working together on a joint project. Many people achieve this by suggesting alphabetical rather than rank listing according to work effort or merit. The first author listed is always assumed to be the senior author, the leader, who has both directed the project and contributed the most. If you are serious about achieving this way, it would even pay to have your surname changed by deed poll to one beginning with the letter A.

An alternative ploy is to let everyone else do all the work and then come in at the last moment and claim that no-one informed you of meetings, you were always willing to help, they were trying to impede your career by not informing you of what needed to be done, and that you are going to the managing director over this blatant case of discrimination. Such tactics have been known to succeed in getting a person's name on a report when there has been no input whatever! Of course, you will not be liked for it, but such is the tactic.

THE 'TRUE BLUE' WAY

However, successful achievers usually do it the hard way. While they are very much aware that it pays to 'win friends and influence people', they are prepared to put in the time, energy, commitment and dedication to earn the promotions and to feel proud of their achievements. They also try to ensure that their reputations remain intact. Not for them the short-cuts to promotion. They want to earn the respect of their families, friends, colleagues and competitors.

Like it or not, most women in the new environment of equal opportunity and affirmative action will still have to earn promotion, and this can be made easier by being aware of the criteria involved in the 'credentialling' process. Specifically, most future achievers will have the right educational credentials. This will apply whether you are a woman or a man. A Bachelor's degree is usually a requirement for a management job, no matter what the industry. This is because technological change means that organisations need people who have been trained to think rather than rely on 'gut feeling' or contacts. Women have been known to overachieve in the educational sphere. Education degrees may be correct for teaching, but are of little use in business unless you wish to remain in the training and development area. So target your job and industry and make sure that your tertiary credentials are in line with the target.

You may believe that the secretarial path is still a possible route into management or that you do not need a degree; what really counts is experience on the job. While this may occasionally be so, we are talking about top management. The days when the top echelon did not need to have credentials are drawing to a close, mainly because they will soon not be able to talk to their 'high-tech' subordinates. Moreover, even the humble but essential secretary can now improve her status by taking business degrees with a secretarial/administration major. There is no need to stay in the role of a traditional secretary unless you especially wish to. Opportunities now exist to move into broader fields, depending on qualifications and inclination.

You may be distressed to learn that you should marry your qualifications to your career. What happened to academic freedom, to intellectual development? Isn't it the training that is important, rather than the nomenclature? Well, most organisations have a vocational bent and prefer people who can 'fit in' with alacrity. Nowadays the economic climate is tougher and competition is too great to spend time on re-training. A vocationally-oriented credential takes preference, in most cases, over ones that 'broaden the mind'. Organisations want people who can produce, not intellectualise about something which is not relevant to everyday operations. If you are truly ambitious then you will ensure that you get your qualifications early and in the right areas.

Another significant 'credentialling' process is management training —both at work and through formal courses. Most women receive little training in management. In fact, the same applies to men. They are a subordinate one day, and a manager the next, and expected to perform with the wisdom of Solomon! However, men do receive in-house training in management, or are sent to external training institutions to overcome 'deficiencies' in certain areas. The same opportunities are now only just being provided for women. The *Women in Management* study found that only a small number of women were being given this type of training, and usually in areas like human relations. Given that women are acknowledged as being more sympathetic, the choice of courses seems a little strange. It is just another example of the male managerial culture judging needs and wants according to outdated criteria.

If your organisation does not provide management training, don't complain—*do something about it yourself.* There are numerous outside organisations, like the Australian Institute of Management, or even Women And Management, who provide short and inexpensive courses for women in the relevant areas. Alternatively, make representations to your organisation to be given such training. You may be surprised by the result; they may have been waiting for you to show an interest so that they could accelerate your career. (Hierarchies often think that women are not interested in management or in taking responsibility). Moreover, try to face the 'dragons' we all like to avoid: those ubiquitous finance, accounting and computer courses. Having once jumped this hurdle you may find that you actually like these areas and develop a whole new career path for yourself.

You must also acquire a more important commodity—management experience on the job. It is no good expecting to reach senior management if you have not established a track record in managing large departments or divisions, in facing industrial relations disputes (and winning), handling budgets and earning profits, creating organisational change, firing staff when the need arises, and being the boss of large numbers of people. Without this experience you will not be able to cope, will have little respect from your colleagues, subordinates and foes, and will undermine the chances of the women who are lining up to follow you.

So forget the women's ghettos: those cosy areas where you all get great satisfaction from each other and the work at hand. Go off into the mainstream, and earn your 'brownie points'. The rewards will be there in the end!

7

How to manage your family, dog, cat, and so on . . .

FEW WOMEN MANAGERS these days are alone. In fact, their lives differ enormously from the stereotypical image of the spinster in sombre suit and glasses, returning to her solitary bed-sitter after a hard day's work at the office.

Modern management women have homes, apartments, husbands, lovers, live-in companions, marriage contracts, children, step-children, nannies, housekeepers, au-pair girls, aged parents, poor relations, deserving friends, cats, dogs, budgies, gardens, and assorted other forms of responsibility.

The question then arises: how do they manage all this and still have a career? Are they superwomen or are they just average, but with constantly frayed nerves? How to they do all this and still pursue a demanding career?

The answer is simple: *they just do it.* How? Most manage their domestic responsibilities in the same way they organise their offices. The home, or life away from the office, has become an extension of the office.

This may not be common knowledge, but the extended office has replaced the extended family. Modern management techniques have infiltrated the home, which is now synonymous with routines, procedures, deadlines, computerised shopping lists, job rotation, job segmentation, union (family) demarcation, strikes, machinery malfunctions, technological innovation, technological obsolescence, servicemen, financial advisers, home entertaining, the home office, computer modems to tap into the computer at work, and networked computer terminals should you stray too far from base. The age of innovation has caught up with that most traditional and sacred of rituals—the domestic routine.

Women should no longer complain. Their roles as children's caretaker, nurse, family counsellor, scrubbing woman, gardener, housekeeper, and family treasurer can now be *delegated* (just like the office). Top career women are skilled in the art of delegation. *They don't want to be in control of everything*—an artificial situation which makes some women feel important. They want to achieve and the best way to do that is to organise and then delegate.

If you're skeptical about this, and wondering how the home can be organised, when you have three children under three, one on the way, your husband doesn't help, you don't have relatives that help, and you go to work—remember that you have two choices. Either get organised by whatever means you have within your power, or have a nervous breakdown!

Anyone who believes that such organisation is impossible ('No-one understands my problem') is not really serious about a career. She just likes to daydream about it, to imagine how it would be, when all the time she is content to do other things. Unhappily, she then uses these other things as the reason for her non-achievement. The complainers need to be more honest. Instead of looking for excuses, they should examine their own motivation.

So you either want a career or are content with a demanding domestic life. You can't maintain both. However, by making modifications to your lifestyle, you can organise your domestic life to allow for a demanding career. The following advise is for those who are prepared to do this.

THE MARRIAGE CONTRACT

Just as many people now have formalised employment contracts—of fixed term, with binding conditions of responsibilities and perks—so marriage or its more modern version, cohabitation, has come of age. Those wise enough to negotiate a marriage contract before entering into partnership seem to prosper when the initial euphoria disappears. Others are forced to bear all the penalties when a break-up occurs. The old saying *caveat emptor* (let the buyer beware) still applies in these modern times. A marriage contract seems to be a necessity of life, along with bread, bank loans and credit cards!

Given that romance now has contractual strings attached, what should be contained in such a contract? Practitioners of this safeguard act tend to enshrine the 50-50 principle. Kay, aged 38 and managing director of a media-oriented company, explains:

> Paul and I have been living together for five years. Before that, we had both had lots of affairs. Because I wanted a career, I was determined that he and I would share the housework. I was not going to work all day and then come home and start all over again while he either did nothing or was out enjoying himself. So I proposed a contract before I agreed to live with him. I must admit this rather surprised him, but he didn't put up much resistance. After I explained why (my mother had been left to fend for herself, my sister and I), we talked about terms and had a proper contract drawn up by a solicitor. Neither of us has regretted it. And it has saved a lot of arguments.
>
> For instance, we share everything 50-50. We bought this house 50-50. We share the chores 50-50. If I cook one night, he cooks the other while I wash up. He does the washing one time, and I do it the other. He puts the garbage out one week, and I do it the next. If one of us misses out because we may be away on business, we either double up or do something else for the other.
>
> At the commencement we had to work out rosters because we would forget who had done what—particularly if we had been having a bad week. Now it is so routine that we don't need pieces of paper. At times Paul rebelled, especially if he wanted to go out with the boys. However, he's found lots of new talents. For instance, he's a good cook (much better than I am), he loves entertaining, and he is also better at housework that I am. On the other hand, I have discovered that I am good at organising the budget, the bills, the loan repayments and other financial matters. In fact, this new discovery led me to go on and try for top jobs. I wasn't such a dummy after all—especially when it came to money! Paul is very proud of me for that.
>
> Some of my women friends try to sympathise with him, saying how could I do this to him—that is, keep him doing household chores with a contract. They tell him that if he were theirs, they would look after him. But he just laughs—thank goodness. I would

hate to have to break in another man now that the practice is working. I must admit I had my own doubts at first—I used to feel so guilty when he was trying to cook—but not any more. It is a nice feeling to come home after a hard day's work to a nice cooked meal and a glass of wine. I might have to do it the next night, but it is worthwhile just to be able to relax the other night. I believe that our relationship is the stronger for this approach because we both have a chance to relax and are not so snappy with each other.

This is an unusual story and an unusual couple. Both are hard-headed business people, yet recognise the validity of business methods in the home. Despite an occasional emotional reaction, the logic of the business methodology has survived. However, the real success of the story lies in the fact that they ignore traditional role traps. Kay has learned to fix cars, tinker with the tricky lawn mower and change light bulbs. Paul can sew on a button, and iron his shirt. If either is away for any length of time, the other is able to handle any emergency without feeling lost, incapable or inadequate. The contract has made both more self-sufficient, while at the same time cementing the foundations for a real partnership and a dual career family.

The contract works for Kay and Paul, but may not work for you. There is a definite 50-50 split, even to who makes up the bed each morning. Both are fortunate in finding the other agreeable to the arrangement. If you are half-hearted, or let your vigilance slip, then it will not work. The contract will be irredeemable, and may also mark the end of the relationship.

NANNIES

Unlike Kay, some women executives have young children. How do they cope? Is it possible to combine children and career? Pamela, aged 35, a busy executive with three young children all under five, and an equally busy executive husband, relates her story:

We manage in our family by employing lots of nannies. At present we have four working for us. Because Rod and I have to leave so early in the morning, there is a girl who comes in and gets the children up, bathes them, and then gives them their breakfast. She then goes off to Uni, and our day nanny arrives for the day. She takes the oldest one off to pre-school three times a week, and looks after the others while Rod and I are at work. Another lass arrives in the late afternoon to look after the children until one or other of us gets home from work. If neither of us are going to be there because we have a function to attend or are away interstate, then another will come in and stay overnight. This last one will also babysit if we have problems at weekends.

It was hard trying to get things organised at first with so many girls, but the system works well now. The children are never alone. I also have a lady who comes in during the week to do the cleaning, washing and ironing. The total arrangement costs a lot of money, but both Rod and I earn good salaries and I am able to keep my career. I have only had a few weeks off with each pregnancy and have kept on going. The nanny system has enabled me to do that.

Some people have criticised me for the arrangement. But the children are not deprived, and know that Rod and I are their parents. They think it is perfectly normal that their mother goes to work. I'm trying to do my bit for the next generation, and I hope my girls will also have a career.

Pamela had the usual guilt feelings when she first left her children for her career. However, she was in the process of establishing herself and a dormant period would have meant the end of any real achievement. Not content to be an 'also ran', she and her husband came up with the solution—relays of nannies! It is a creative solution and an affordable one in the majority of two-income households.

LABOUR SAVERS

Other married women have other solutions. Schooled in more traditional moulds, they like to have their careers and still do all the housework. How do they manage? Maureen found this solution when visiting a friend:

An old school friend had invited me home to dinner. I didn't particularly want to go because I knew she was a very busy person. But she insisted, and I'm glad I went. I had a real education. Her home was technology gone mad. I have never seen so many gadgets, all designed to cut down her effort. 'Labour saving devices' her husband proudly said, while he sat there doing nothing. He didn't need to be involved. He just paid for the latest toy, while she whipped around the place managing everything in double quick time. She had everything; all the latest things on the market. She was a retailer's pride and joy!

For instance, the meal was cooked by microwave oven and washed up in the dishwasher. While we were talking idly afterwards, she ironed the week's clothes on a small portable Elna dry-cleaner's press which did the ironing in a fraction of the time. Of course she also had the appropriate washing machines, dryers and other paraphernalia.

The home was run by technological wizardry. The air-conditioning came on at appropriate times; external blinds lowered themselves to cut out the western sun; bells rang mysteriously to signal the commencement or finish of some routine operation in the house; the swimming pool was covered by mesh cover which rolled back at the press of a button; and down in the basement there was a huge train set which she, her husband and two daughters used to relax with after the 'chores' were done. In fact, I was inducted to this marvel for a certain period of time.

Her husband was very proud of her efficiency—aided by the labour saving devices. If there was a gadget to help her, then she had it. No-one else did anything, except respond to the routine that she had established.

I must admit it was a bit regimented. When I arrived the girls played the piano for me for five minutes; then the husband showed off his latest stereo equipment (the best I had ever seen) for five minutes; we had a drink for five minutes; we had the air-conditioning turned on for five minutes; we sat at the dining table and had our entree for five minutes; we then waited five minutes while the main meal cooked in the micro-wave; we then ate that in five minutes; and so on. I may sound extreme and critical, but that is how it felt to an outsider. Everything ran like clockwork and she felt very proud of her accomplishments. She is the only person I know to successfully combine career, marriage, home and family. She was on the run the whole time (she has always been a very energetic person), but she managed to *do everything herself*. I was impressed; and also felt a little inferior that I had not had the sense to work out something like that myself.

Alas, not everyone is in the financial position to afford this particular lifestyle, or they may not also have a husband who likes technological gadgets. Most homes these days have many of these things although they may not run as efficiently as that of Maureen's friend. Perhaps there is a lesson to be learned about the transfer of management skills. Maureen's friend apparently made the transition: why not other women?

Of course, if you are not prepared for order and efficiency, then expect your home to be chaotic. Efficiency may seem plastic and sterile, but top career women are always on the lookout for ways to increase their effectiveness. A little management skill may help you to survive in your increasingly overworked world!

STILL AT HOME

The case of Yvonne, aged 36 and a very ambitious executive, may be of interest to unmarried career aspirants:

> Lots of people think I am crazy because I still live at home. But I wouldn't be able to manage my career if I didn't. Mum and Dad are both retired, and spend most of their day looking after me. I may be at work, but they are kept busy looking after my 'other' life—the one away from the office!
>
> For example, I leave very early in the morning and don't get home most nights until late. There is always a meeting to go to, or a function of one sort or another. I am just so busy that I couldn't sustain a marriage. So it is just as well that I have Mum and Dad to back me up on the home front, while my secretary looks after me at work.
>
> For years now Mum has been my home secretary. People are always trying to contact me, either at work or at home. Mum has a good arrangement with my secretary—they both manage my life—and in fact keep me in contact with people. If I am not at the office, my secretary will leave messages with Mum and vice-versa. Mum will also do investigations for me, apart from looking after my meals, dressmaking for me and other womanly chores.
>
> Dad often acts as my chauffeur, and handles all my financial matters. I just don't have time to even go to the bank, so he handles that. If there are bills to pay, I just write out the necessary documentation and he does the work. He will return things for me, get my shoes mended, even do my shopping. I never go to the stores—don't have time—so someone has to do it. We are a team, the three of us, and they, along with my secretary, are very involved in my life.
>
> It is hard for other people to understand because they don't realise the extent of the demands in my job. I would be lost without the family, because I would not be able to do the job and the other chores as well. If I didn't have Mum and Dad, then I would have to employ a home secretary, housekeeper, gardener, dressmaker, and chauffeur. One day I may have to. But at the moment it is nice to have them so involved and active. They enjoy it because they feel they are making a contribution to the well-being of the home and career. It is not just my career, it is also theirs. It is a team effort, and we all share in the losses and successes.

This is another unusual case, but this time the family manages, or is an important extension of, the executive. The arrangement is satisfactory to all and keeps four people (including the office secretary) busy and involved. Of course, Yvonne is not married or involved in a relationship, and she has no children. The career is the all consuming passion and has taken over four people's lives. This often happens to men: why not to women? However, everyday chores still have to be done and if the woman is the career person then someone else has to do them. Yvonne has found her solution and kept a home life with her parents.

BUT MY LIFE IS NORMAL!

None of these situations apply to you. Your life is normal, with normal routines. You just want to know what to do when there is a small 'hiccup'. How do you manage when you suddenly have to go away interstate for a few nights?

Well, there are a number of possibilities, permutations and combinations. Consider the following sample:

- hire a babysitter;
- ask your mother, father, sister, brother, etc. to move in and play 'mother', 'housekeeper';
- ask a friend to perform the same function;
- shut the house, and either ask the neighbours to look after the animals or put them in a nearby kennel;
- shut the house, and take the family with you;
- shut the house, and lodge the family at your mother's;
- any variation on the above.

Should you have to travel overseas for any length of time, you can:

- ask or pay a friend or member of the family to babysit the house and animals;
- shut the house and lodge the animals in a kennel;
- move the family into your mother's;
- move the family into your mother-in-law's;
- have your mother or mother-in-law move in;
- have your husband or the children trained to take over;
- leave everything to your partner or companion;
- arrange for Neighbourhood Watch to keep an eye on things;

- arrange for 'Angels' to come and water the plants, feed the animals and generally look after things;
- arrange for a reliable housekeeper;
- any variation on the above.

These are ordinary solutions to ordinary problems. The important thing to realise is that if you wish to have a career, you will just have to manage these other aspects of your life.

THE CRUNCH

However, with increasing seniority and responsibility in your career some more serious decisions may have to be made. For instance, no matter what you do your partner may not be sympathetic to your career ambitions. It is him or you. A crisis has been reached. How can you maintain your career? You can:

- divorce him (if married);
- leave him (if living together);
- declare a moratorium, a 'cooling off' period (in more fashionable circles, a 'temporary' separation);
- have a frank discussion with him—he either understands or he leaves;
- live in separate parts of the house;
- cut off his allowance (if keeping him)
- send him home to mother (if keeping him)
- have a nervous breakdown (your career will falter);
- cry (he will still be the same);
- get someone to explain your nature to him;
- go to marriage guidance counselling;
- give in (he expects it!);
- lower your career ambitions (he expects it because he can't compete!);
- change your job (he expects it);
- stop work altogether and live on him (he *doesn't* expect that and will probably leave you!);
- take advice from others who have been in similar situations;

- learn to ignore him, and let him sort out his own problems;
- solve his career problems first, and then work on yours—together
- find someone else who is happy about your career.

Alternatively, you may have children who are equally unrespon-sive to your career ambitions. Ruined by your indulgent attention in your earlier days, they cannot comprehend why you insist on having a 'career'. They are not prepared to give up their satisfactory lifestyles (where you do all the work for them) to accommodate your needs. There is no 'give and take'—it is all take! Faced with such a situation, and still determined about your career, you can:

- leave them (many a famous woman has had to take that drastic step);
- talk to them and try to come to an arrangement where you are given some time for yourself;
- have a nervous breakdown (they will be too selfish to look after you);
- cry (they won't be home to see it);
- work out routines for the family and insist they stick to them;
- cut off their allowances (if keeping them);
- off-load them on various relatives;
- send them overseas;
- send them to boarding school;
- hire a housekeeper and lock yourself in your 'den';
- just leave home for several days and see what happens;
- don't attempt a career (that's what they want anyway);
- enlist your husband's help in keeping control of the family—that is, it's your turn for a career;
- get the oldest ones to look after the youngest ones;
- come to an agreement to let you have 'your chance' for a number of years;
- go back to school, get an education, and continue regardless;
- disregard the noise, clutter, and disorder and let life sort itself out as it comes;
- talk to other women who have had similar experiences;
- take leave of absence from your job while you sort out the family;

- sort out the family's career problems first, and then tackle your own;

- involve the family in your career so that they will come to understand the pressures;

- write a book on your experiences in trying to have a career.

Another possible complication is if you have been a single career woman for some time and you suddenly meet *the* man. You are faced with the prospect of trying to combine marriage and career. You can:

- give up your career and settle for being wife and mother;

- postpone having children for a while (it may become too late);

- have children immediately and re-enter the workforce as soon as you can;

- have children and hire nannies (remember Pamela?);

- hire a housekeeper, nanny, and any other necessary help;

- get your mother (or mother-in-law) to live with you;

- take the baby to work (some women have been known to do this);

- work from home;

- work part-time;

- help your husband in his work, career, profession;

- ask other women what they have done;

- live apart (some women have done this);

- any variation on the above.

THE CAVEAT

It is important to remember that women executives, and top ones, are *normal* people in that they have the same doubts, fears, troubles, triumphs, successes, prejudices and jealousies as the next person—male or female. The other thing they have, which clearly everyone else does *not* have, is a desire for a career, and a determination to pursue it.

Despite the alarming divorce rate, women *can* combine marriage with a career. It may involve finding a sympathetic male, but even the most cantankerous have been known to mellow as a woman becomes more successful. In fact, some have even become *proud* and become the woman's best public relations officer!

Other women have faced their hurdles and established careers in the face of overwhelming odds. They have triumphed in spite of everything. Many of these have maintained their marriages; those who haven't have gone on to establish better relationships with others. Some have chosen to divorce or to remain single. Most acknowledge that their lifestyle is better for the choices they have made.

Women's desire for family is normal, it is here to stay. So if given the opportunity to combine career and family, then take it. But remember, that it will all have to be managed. And that is what distinguishes a top woman manager from the rest—she knows how to manage!

8

Five corporate women

MOST TOP WOMEN managers have either succeeded within the corporate environment or have started their own businesses. Far more is known about those who have succeeded in the corporate world. The women entrepreneurs/proprietors are a 'new breed', a recent development in 'liberation politics'. Driven by a lack of job satisfaction and low employment status, the female entrepreneur has ventured out on her own to satisfy her need to achieve, her desire to be independent, and, sometimes, out of sheer economic necessity. Researchers have only lately become aware of this phenomenon as more women opt for independence. Consequently, this 'new breed' is ill defined and somewhat mysterious. However, starting your own business is becoming a viable alternative for ambitious women, offering a way round the seemingly impenetrable barriers.

Successful corporate and entrepreneurial women have many things in common. For instance, they are usually well educated (there are a few exceptions), have a very supportive family or spouse (partner), are first-born children or the first girl in the family, have high achievement needs, and work in service-related industries.

However, the two groups face dissimilar problems. Corporate women have to survive in the corporate 'jungle' and have different responsibilities to those in the outside world. For instance, they may not have to raise finance or negotiate new business. However, they do have to traverse the committee or meeting structures, compete for scarce resources against their male colleagues, and also earn a profit (otherwise they become unemployable). They also have to manage teams of people and accept responsibility for their successes and failures.

The issues involved in being a 'corporate' woman have been well documented in earlier chapters. What we have not yet revealed is how corporate women perceive their careers and their experiences. Like many variations on a theme, there are many 'herstories' of corporate women. They do not all necessarily conform, either to one another or to all the ground rules laid down in this book. The following case studies illustrate some of the permutations and combinations in the career success factor.

Joan Playford*

Many women think they cannot succeed in a male dominated company. Joan has not only proven this wrong, she has also succeeded in a non-traditional occupation. She has only worked for the one company, yet she has succeeded in becoming one of the top management group.

The youngest of three children, Joan was born some nine years after her brother who was the middle child. Both her father and brother were engineers, while her sister was good at mathematics. Joan was educated in public schools, going to an opportunity school in her last two years in primary and then on to Sydney's Fort Street Girl's High (where she came under the influence of the legendary Headmistress, Fanny Cohen). She went on to Sydney University in the mid-1950s to study for a science degree, majoring in mathematics and physics.

On obtaining her degree she was at a loss as to what to do. A casual conversation with a fellow graduate at a New Year's Eve party resulted in her ringing up her future employer to enquire about a job. The executive who answered her call responded that they did not employ female graduate trainees. He happened to relate this conversation at morning tea, only to be told by a more senior executive to 'get the girl in'. Following an interview Joan was offered a job and has been with the company ever since, apart from a two-year sabbatical when she went to Harvard University to do an MBA (at her own expense).

During her 26 years with the company, Joan has performed many job functions, including personnel, and in the early years even faced what could now be called discriminatory treatment. However, she managed to weather this and her present position now places her among the top twelve senior executives in the company. Her job is highly responsible and involves considerable negotiating to settle supplies and prices of energy for three-year periods. She is the most senior woman; there is a big gap, hierarchically, between Joan and other women in the organisation.

She comments on her career, her style of management and why she has stayed so long in the one company:

> There are a lot of things about this company that fit in with my personality. Besides being conservative, which I am also, it is in a line of business that I can identify with. I couldn't work for a company that made cigarettes. I don't think I would be too enthusiastic about Kleenex tissues either. But I can be enthusiastic about energy; it is a very important thing. The company has a good attitude towards its people in general, is a little old fashioned from time to time, but is a very reputable organisation.
>
> I was in the company fourteen years before I went to Harvard. I used to spend a lot of time on outside activities—like the Hockey Association and amateur theatricals, Sunday School and Youth Camps. Perhaps I should have had more ambition earlier on, but there were no other women, apart from a woman supervisor, to provide competition, act as role models or make me think, 'Gee, I can do that too'. I don't think I had any aspirations before I went off to Harvard and I only went there because I was feeling 'browned off'. But Harvard gave me a boost in confidence. After that I began to think of my job as a career, rather than just a job.
>
> My present job is fantastic. I work with very interesting people. The negotiating part itself is exciting, challenging and mentally stimulating. But it is also very exhausting because we have to do a lot of travelling for about eighteen months when we negotiate the new pricing agreement every three years. The travelling just wrecks your social life. However, I have some skills that are important in the negotiating role; I am both patient and logical. You can't afford to be impatient. We have a small negotiating team—three or four of us—and we have to work long hours. The pressure is really on; twelve- to sixteen-hour days are not unusual, and then you travel home for the weekend and go back again on

Monday. You just keep going during those times, but I don't think it is a good life.

As a manager I basically work on the principle that if I expect people to do things they will do them. Most of the time this doesn't present a problem. However, the difficult part comes when you have to dress someone down for not doing what you want them to do. The trick is to find some way to do that without turning them off. I find that quite challenging. The other challenging thing is getting people to work towards the same goal. People have different values and personalities and may not necessarily believe in the same things that I do. What I take for granted—like working a full day—they may not have in their value system.

I suppose I have certain expectations. For instance, I expect people to tell me what is going on in their areas, especially if it affects mine, and I tell others about my area. I get upset when people don't tell me and something goes wrong. I am pretty blunt when that happens. I have told a few of my peers off from time to time for that. I don't think I like to have a fight but I am in a job where I fight all day. I stand up for my rights and if I think I am getting a raw deal. I also say my piece if someone in my area is being poorly treated. Before I became more ambitious I used to let people walk all over me; I don't do that much now.

Women tend to grow up wanting to be liked, needing to be accepted. Therefore you don't tend to expect to dominate just for domination's sake. But I am continually amused at some of my male colleagues who, just because of their position in the company, expect to be able to throw their weight around.

Men and women differ too in the way they react to, or accept, things. For instance, I could have had a company parking spot for about four or five years now, but I just chose to come to work by train because I didn't own a car. You would not believe the pressure that people put on me to buy a car to use that parking spot. At the beginning of the year I did buy a car because I could benefit from a company discount. Since then I have been driving, and using the car parking spot. Everyone has now breathed a sigh of relief because I am conforming to what they think is important.

I also run into other problems because I like to play cards. I have been playing cards for years, especially with the fellows in the canteen. I think the General Manager has a problem with that. I feel you should get to know as many people as possible and that is one way to do it. It helps you build a support system, and if you want to know something or get some gossip all you have to do then is ring someone up. There are only sixteen to twenty people playing cards, but it is a reasonable network to relate to.

Several people have influenced me over time. My headmistress was a dominating influence; then there were several executives in this company whom I enjoyed working for and who gave good advice; and one of the ministers of our church (I went out with his son for six years).

I think my family has always taken it for granted that I would achieve but not necessarily in the business world. In the family, mother has been the dominating force although father had the brains. My grandmother was also a dominant woman, like her mother before her. Women are the dominating ones in the family generally. My mother, although 80, is very supportive and my greatest fan. She has always expected me to do well. If I came home and said, 'Mum, I got a promotion', she would reply and say, 'Yes, well, that is what I expected'.

I have had to learn a lot of things about managing during my career. First of all I had to learn confidence. I think it is funny when I look back because at school I had no trouble being prefect, house captain and running whatever was required. Yet when it came to the work environment I just didn't have the same confidence.

Then I had to learn not to feel that when someone disagreed with me they were criticising me as a person. Rather they were disagreeing with the idea or thing I wanted to do. As women we tend to see any form of criticism as a rejection of ourselves as people. I have had to learn to take criticism without taking it as outright rejection.

I don't think I have ever been a radical woman's opportunist, but there is no doubt that the social changes have had an impact on my life. I don't think I would be where I am today without them. There would have been no reason for this company to change its stance if it hadn't become aware of the changing times. Interestingly, I was interviewed by a large newspaper and they did a terrible job at reporting the interview. I had made some comments about older directors, and about how younger men might accept women more because their wives worked. The reporter messed it up. The result was that I received a telephone call from the Chairman of the Board! At the time I was highly embarrassed, but in hindsight it was probably good for me. At least he had become aware of me, whereas I don't think he even knew I existed previously!

Joan began her career when there were not so many opportunities for women. Nevertheless, she has been a 'front-runner' and has broken many barriers for women in a technical and male-dominated world. Although she realises that her career would probably have been different if starting out today, she has a great sense of achievement and feels she is contributing something worthwhile to her organisation and society. As she herself puts it: 'I have a need to be appreciated and people appreciate me. Therefore, I feel a sense of achievement. I feel I have been very lucky really'.

Jane Thompson*

Aged 45 and an Associate Director in a large market research company, Jane was introduced in Chapter 2. She was born in a Victorian country town, the middle child in a family of seven children. Not long afterwards the family moved to Melbourne, where her father worked as a tram driver. The family was poor financially, but rich in parental love. Jane left school at the age of fifteen after being educated in convent schools. The family could only afford to educate the four sons; the three girls left school after attaining the minimum qualification.

Jane had three jobs before having her first child at the age of 25 (she married at 24). The last job was quite responsible, being the office manager for a retail chain which was owned by a former Lord Mayor of Melbourne and a City Councillor. Jane also helped her boss with some of his Council work.

After the birth of her first child she became a surburban housewife. Another child followed two years later. Her husband, a marketing executive, then began to get 'itchy feet' and the couple eventually bought a newsagency in a Victorian country town. They both worked in the business for four years, until Jane again became pregnant. Her husband then decided that the time was right for another move as Jane would have to leave the business and the additional wage costs for her replacement would make the agency less viable financially. They returned to Melbourne; he to his old profession and she to looking after the children and her father, who was now a widower.

She began her eventual career and rise to success this way:

> When my third child was not quite two I started to become a bit bored with just being a housewife. I mentioned to my husband that I would like to look for a job. He pooh-poohed the idea, said that it was quite out of the question, that I should be happy to stay at home with the children and do the mother's club bit. I forgot about it for a while until one day a lady doing a market research survey knocked on my door. I invited her in because she had a child with her in a pusher. In fact, I was quite surprised to see a woman working accompanied by her child.
>
> It turned out that her husband was a dentist. He had had to borrow a lot of money to get through his course and to set himself

up. During his studies they had married and the child quickly followed. She was doing this market research work to help pay the bills.

Her experience made me think that maybe this was something I could do. I felt it would be very hard to get back into office work and run a family at the same time. One day I asked my father to come around and mind the children and I went along to her firm for an interview (she had given me a card when she left). They took me on, doing casual work in door-to-door interviewing. I worked for them for four years until my husband took a transfer to Sydney. Actually, I was working almost full-time. I used to be out on the road five days a week and weekends as well. I was a bit sad to leave the job because it gave me pin money, but the Melbourne office told me not to worry—I could do the same work in Sydney.

I contacted the Sydney office after we found a house to live in, and began working again. After a couple of years I became an Area Supervisor with responsibilities for in-field training of interviewers, running a team of fifteen to twenty interviewers in the field, and checking and auditing their work.

I later became New South Wales Field Manager and then National Field Manager. I was appointed an Associate Director twelve months ago. The appointment is a recognition of the contribution that the field force, and especially women, have made to the company.

I'm glad I have a career because my husband travels a lot in his job — in fact, he is overseas about four to five months in the year. My children are growing up, and are either in their last year of school or at University. I have a cleaning person come in every week and a house full of mod-cons. The children think it is great that mum has a career! Even though I don't spend much time with them now, we all sit down to dinner when we can and talk. There is no television in our house. My husband and I will talk till about 10 or 11 o'clock. It's important to communicate. Despite the fact that we are all busy, I try to give the family 'quality' time!

In my present position I am involved in managing women at all levels. There are women State Managers, women Supervisors, women working in the field. In fact, the industry is dominated by women. I have to try and lead and motivate the management people so that they can lead and motivate the people under them. From time to time, problems naturally arise. Fortunately, some of the problems I have had in the past are now gone—hair-raising problems like people stabbing you in the back, and telling lies about you. The latter was a woman I worked for at one stage. I used to go home from work incensed and at screaming point because of the things she did. She was disloyal, to both staff and management, was vindictive, and was trying to claw her way up in the company. Her behaviour eventually proved to be her own undoing, but by that time I had bypassed her and it didn't matter.

When you have a lot of women working together you can get a lot of in-fighting. Our Field Department is a fairly good and happy group. The Coding women fight like cats and dogs at different times. The Data Processing ladies have their ups and downs— there is a great big room full of women sitting at machines all day. We also have one or two negative people who are tops at their job, but as they become older are beginning to change—I think they feel the pressure from the younger women.

Sometimes the pressure in the job has got on top of me. At one stage I was utterly frustrated and the doctor told me that I would end up with an ulcer the way I was going. So I decided that was not going to happen. Nowadays, I don't let the pressure show—I have learnt to do that. But the pressure is always there; something has to be done, it isn't being done, there is only so much time to do it. But if you are not going to be able to do it or get it done by someone, then there is no good getting yourself het up inside.

I plan my day. It is the last thing I do at night. I make out a list, putting at the top the things that have to absolutely be done next day. I also try to keep an ongoing plan because there are priorities in the future that have to be met.

I need the plan because half my day is taken up with people coming in and out of my office or I have to go to meetings. I usually start working early in the morning and take a lot of work home with me. With my husband being away so much I can do that. I get a lot of reports and memos, instructions to State Offices etc., written at night. I don't need a lot of sleep, in fact, never have, even as a child.

When my husband comes home I have to reorganise myself. It is a bit of a joke amongst my colleagues. However, he fully understands because he is a workaholic himself. He gets to work early in the morning because he is a morning person. He knows I am a night person. He gets home before me and will cook the tea. We have dual roles now. He now recognises that my role is equal to his.

He didn't always feel this way, but is now quite proud of what I have achieved. I try to organise my travel away from home around his travel plans. He always knows well in advance so we can work it out. If sometimes it clashes, then my mother-in-law will move in and look after the family or I can always send the boys off to one of my brothers and sisters. That's an advantage of coming from a large family!

I must admit, however, that it is difficult trying to be a career woman and do the mother bit, particularly in today's world. The business demands will not really allow you to have a home life. I feel that is a little harsh, in fact, you shouldn't let business interfere with home life. But it does. A number of women managers I know have swapped roles with their husbands. The women are doing the work bit, while the husband looks after the children and the home. It all depends on how ambitious people are and who has the chance for the best career.

One of the advantages of being an Associate Director is that you are more accepted and recognised within the company. I now get invited to this and that, I am included in lots of things, and my opinions are called for. Previously, this was not the case. However, I still talk to the people in my area because their jobs are not easy—they are meeting deadlines all the time. It is no good me sitting up in my little office, tucked away in Director's Alley, sending them memos to do this and that. I've got to make sure I can still talk to them. So I still go out and buy my lunch and sit with them at lunch time. I'm making sure that they still know that they can talk to me and that I'm always there. I don't just want to hear the good things; I want to know the bad things as well.

I think because I have been there I know what it is like and although I don't want to be there now, if I didn't keep contact with my people, we would soon have problems. That is the type of industry we are in. Performance would drop. It is extremely important to keep communicating at all times with all levels.

I feel at this stage now that I would like to meet more people in management. I need to belong; to meet other people doing similar things to myself. There are a lot of women in much higher management positions than I and I would like to learn more about them and from them. In one sense I am trying to plan for the future. I suppose I am a fairly late starter, in fact very late with a career, and I have received opportunities that shouldn't have perhaps come with my background—particularly, my lack of education. I think that is the great thing about this company. They give you an opportunity and let you run with it if you want to. But they probably want more from us too. And I would like to do that—make a greater contribution—both for myself and the company. That's my next goal; and I am getting gamer!

Jane believes her lack of tertiary education or formal management training is a disadvantage these days. She plans to do something about it to help her understand some of her day to day problems and to make that greater contribution she so earnestly desires. Everything she has done she has learned the hard way. She now needs formal assistance. In her opinion: 'I now need finishing off'.

Helen Marshall*

The Marketing Director for a publishing firm, Helen is the middle child of a family of seven—two sisters and a brother being older, and another two sisters and a brother being younger. Seven years separate the oldest and the youngest sibling. The family was brought up on a farm on the outskirts of Sydney until the father eventually went bankrupt. She was educated at a co-educational convent school at the primary level, and a public high school 'where there was one person from our family in each year'. Helen was very active in high school, being on the school council, in the debating team, in many sporting activities and other organised events.

Her first work experience was as a management cadet for one of the large Sydney retailing firms. She decided on this route, rather than going on to University, because she had always been a 'trader'.

> I had been financially independent from the age of eight or nine, because with such a large family if you wanted anything extra you had to earn it. So I used to go and pick peas, and sell things out of the back-yard. I sold my brother's engine, and worse, my father's overcoat! There was an old building in our street which had been demolished. I took all the electrical wiring and stripped off the plastic and sold the copper wire in the middle for about threepence. I also sold guinea pigs.
>
> During fifth and sixth forms I worked on weekends in a restaurant, and in an office in Sydney during my school holidays. It was a bit of a holiday for me to come to Sydney, earn some money and spend it. I never looked on it as work.

Her retailing experience was short lived because instead of becoming a buyer she was made a department manager in nursery furniture in one of the suburban stores. 'I couldn't stand it; the kids were peeing in the potties. I thought, "this is not for me".'

The next step at nineteen was as a trainee sales representative on the road, selling to pharmacies and department stores all around New South Wales. She was quite successful because it 'was so unusual to have a female sales rep call that people were very helpful to me'. After three years doing this she moved into the office as an assistant to the Marketing Manager. A series of 'assistant to' jobs followed as various executives left and the organisation chart was reshuffled. Eventually she became the Publicity Officer for one of the Perfume Divisions in the organisation, and then a Product Manager. The latter involved overseas travel to Paris and Italy when she was only 23. However, the most important thing was that, '. . . the General

Manager was a woman of about 40. She had started out as a rep and had worked her way up without the help of the women's movement because it was [after] her time. I got on extremely well with her, became her protégé I guess.'

Changes in management in the holding company of the organisation resulted in Helen changing jobs because she was being paid so little: 'I felt exactly the same as I did when I left home: that, "OK I have learned all this stuff, but now I've got to go and test my wings".'

The next opportunity came in the publishing business, but only because Helen used an unusual approach.

I saw this job in the paper for a publicity officer for this new publishing company that was setting up in Australia. I sent off a telegram to them saying don't make any decisions until you hear from me further. Although I didn't have any experience in publishing, I had good experience in the other areas and thought that my lack of specific industry experience could be an advantage. I proved to be right: I got the job and was the third person employed in the company. There was just the General Manager, his secretary and me. I was told, 'we are launching the company in three month's time, we don't have any customers, we have to build a story to let everyone know we are in town, and we have to get the information around to make sure that everyone knows we are here. We have to have a cocktail party; we must also have a stand at the International Book Festival; there are eight overseas dignitaries coming to help us with the opening'—*and I didn't know what to do!*

So I rang up a few people whose names I had been given (they were in the industry) and asked them to have breakfast with me. I explained that I was new to the industry and needed some help. They all came (they were all males and have taken an interest in my development ever since). The overseas visitors were all heads of companies, so it was important that I succeed. In fact, I had to succeed and to prove that I could do my job very well because it was an international company. Fortunately, we had a big name writer out at the same time on a promotional tour. I managed to get him lots of publicity, and he did a big lecture at Sydney University which was a sell-out. He also had his photo on the front page of *The Australian*, which was pushed under the visitor's doors at their hotels the next morning. The paper stated that the writer was here to help launch the company. So the visitors were very pleased and felt quite comfortable with everything. It was luck in a sense.

That was the beginning of my career with the company. I decided that I should do something different from what other people were doing in the publishing business: in fact, my philosophy is that if it hasn't been done before then that is a good enough reason for you to do it. I have instigated new systems and new marketing programmes in the industry which have been quite successful, and we have also launched a couple of extremely successful ranges of fiction for children—a category which didn't exist before. I was promoted to Marketing Manager last year. At the beginning of this year, the overseas parent company decided to make this company separate and so appointed a Board of Directors. I became a Director for the Australian organisation, along with the National Sales Manager and the Operations Manager. The other person is the Managing Director. That is all the management structure we have because we are a small company. I can honestly say that I was not appointed to the Board as a 'token' woman. In publishing, probably more than any other industry, it doesn't matter whether you are a man or a woman because the people who make the money for you could be either men or women writers. It is what they have written that counts and whether it will sell or not!

I do have a problem though as a woman in this field. The thing I find most difficult is managing people. I'm sure it is lack of experience because basically I have always worked as a loner. I have always wanted to be in a position where I thought up the ideas and other people went out and executed them. I'm not a good detail person. My biggest aim at the moment is to be a good manager. It is very difficult to make the transition. You can't go and learn it anywhere, you can only get guidance about the pitfalls and ways to approach people.

I also made the mistake of assuming that if you leave people alone to do a job they will do it. The hardest thing for me to learn has been that because I can do something not everyone else can. I just assumed that everyone else could do what I could do because I don't have a pecking order on my ability—I think it is because I don't have a tertiary education and haven't learnt about competition between people.

I will probably remain Marketing Director for some time now. But I would like to be Publisher here. We don't have one yet, but when the time comes I want to be ready and prepared.

One thing I have learnt during my career which came as quite a shock is that as I have moved towards more lofty heights the people I have to work with don't necessarily know more than I do. That discovery has been wonderful, because I had assumed they did. All the mystery that surrounds the lofty executive positions is there to protect the people in them. There would probably be a rush if everyone found out how easy it all really is!

Helen feels she is now in a transition period, but also on the brink of a golden opportunity—one which she could easily mess up. However, she remains optimistic because she still does not know what her limitations are. She sums up her feelings about being a career woman thus:

> I never would have been promoted if I had been a radical feminist—that would have just upset everyone. I also don't waltz around here as if I am high and mighty. My advice to women is not to be too concerned with the fact that you are a woman. Forget it. Develop your skills and energies and direct them correctly. Don't expect things to happen overnight and do pay attention to other people who know—who have learned through experience.

Emily Johnson*

Not every woman in the corporate world has a smooth upward path. Sometimes there are many false starts, tangents and 'hiccups' before a career begins to sychronise with fate. However, when a backward look occurs, a steady pattern is discernible. It all depends on how paths are perceived, and what is considered important at various stages in a life.

Emily, aged 37, is now a Group Account Director for one of the large advertising agencies in Sydney. This is a senior position in advertising, one to which a 'glass ceiling' traditionally obstructed women. However, several women have recently been appointed Managing Directors of prominent agencies, so clearly the tide is turning.

Emily, an only child, was born in New Zealand. The family came to Australia when she was five. She went to Vaucluse Public School, followed by Sydney Girls High School and Sydney University, where she obtained a Bachelor of Arts majoring in Psychology, Sociology and Anthropology. She also did a post-graduate year in Clinical and Abnormal Psychology, before getting married and moving to Canada with her husband. They were away for seven years, mostly in Canada but also in London for a while. They arrived back in Australia in 1976. On her return she completed a Master of Commerce degree at the University of New South Wales.

Emily's first job was during her first post-graduate year when she acted as a research assistant to the Psychology Professor.

> I abused that job terribly as I still had a student mentality. I would come in at 10 a.m. and leave at 4 p.m. and have two-hour lunches. It was also the time that my husband was wooing me. I was all terribly distracted by being madly in love and planning to go overseas.
> When we went to England I got a job in market research

because of my research background. However, in Canada jobs were not so easy and I ended up as a Girl Friday—a bit of typing at 30 words a minute and office organisation and administration. I loved the job, but hated the people I had to work for—two rotten men! One had real problems with women—he hated his mother and took it out on every woman he saw. He was a real bastard. I finally took courage in both hands and said I wasn't coming back after my holidays.

I then got back into market research where I remained for nearly three years with a very good company. Then the market research industry went 'bang' and I was laid off along with many others. I went off to do a French course in Montreal because it was becoming increasingly important to have a command of the language. After that I began looking for any job that was remotely connected with market research. My husband suggested trying advertising agencies because they had research departments. So I looked up the Canadian equivalent of the Pink Pages and began ringing around asking people if they had a vacancy in their research department. Eventually this company said, 'No, but our account co-ordinator left to-day'. I said, 'What's an account co-ordinator?' It turned out to be the first step in the account management process in an advertising agency. I was hired, and did the function until the agency decided to move certain sections from Montreal to Toronto because of the English–French political situation which was brewing at that time.

I didn't want to move to Toronto—it was almost like going from Sydney to Melbourne—so the agency offered me other jobs in media and the traffic department, all of which I declined. I finally said, 'Why can't I be an account executive?' The reply was that they had never had a female account executive because the clients would object to such an appointment. The actual words were, 'A guy wouldn't work with a woman and if the client was a female (and we had a few), well, we all know that women can't get on with women!' There were also other arguments like, 'What would you do if a client swore in front of you?' I said, 'I would fall into a dead faint—what do you think? I couldn't care less if he swore'. The argument continued on that level.

It really got heavy and eventually the top guys came from Montreal to Toronto to sort it out. They ended up having a debate with that senior executive for a couple of hours, countering his every argument, and saying, 'Give her a go, of course she can do it', until eventually he said, 'All right, we'll do it', in that tone of voice. You can imagine how much I was under the miscroscope. But surprise, surprise. The client didn't resign the account and I was able to get on with being the first female account executive. I also didn't fall into a faint when they swore at me! I was 24.

Then my husband decided he wanted to move to England. I got a job with Foote, Combe and Belding [advertising agency] when I landed and simply adored it. They thought I was the most fantastic thing since sliced bread, which did wonders for my confidence. I threw myself into that job and got valuable experience. But it was short-lived. My husband pined for Canada, so off we went again. I then worked for two good agencies, both of whom were multi-nationals.

By now I was rising steadily through the ranks—account executive to senior account executive—when my mother became ill and we came back to Australia. I applied for a job with one of the companies I had worked with overseas and they offered me a job as account director. I replied that I had never done that job before (to me an account director was like way up there and how could little Emily do that?) They said that if I didn't tell anyone, then neither would they. I took the job, but in retrospect I was out of my depth. When you are an account director you are heavily involved with strategic planning and I had only done a little of this under guidance from an excellent male superior who was a good role model.

I struggled through my first year but eventually got on top of it. I was then headhunted by another agency and became a senior account director with them. The next stage was Group Account Director and that was when I began to hit barriers. . .there are only about five women in the job [of Group Account Director] in Sydney and most of them are very well known.

It's not that women can't do the job—its just that this is where the prejudice barrier begins. The job is at the level where you have complete responsibility for running the accounts. You report straight through to a Director of Client Services or the Managing Director but only on a needs basis. You also have three to four people working for you, most of whom will be male, and that's another problem. You are also dealing with Marketing Directors and Managing Directors as clients, who may or may not feel comfortable about dealing with a woman. It is the level of responsibility and the status and the power that creates the problem. A lot of companies can't conceive the idea of putting a woman into that position.

I had joined my last agency on the promise that I would be made a Group Account Director. It didn't eventuate. At this stage, we had another change in our life. We decided to go to New Zealand for a quieter life. My mother was dying and I think I was really looking for an escape; I didn't want to face the idea of her dying. We loved it in New Zealand for five months, and then I learned something important about myself. The whole pace of life there is so slow that we calmed down and down until I literally felt like my brain was going to sleep, contracting, and I felt I would forget how to think. It was an unnerving feeling. So we came back to Australia.

I rejoined my previous agency in a new area which was looking at future trends. It was absolutely fascinating. It was like a marketing consultancy within the advertising agency. I did specialist projects for new clients and existing clients—looking for new market potential, market gaps, re-positioning of existing products. However, at this time I also decided to have a baby. I was getting close to being 35 and if I didn't have a child soon I wouldn't have one. I fell pregnant, obtained leave of absence from the agency and came back three months after my daughter was born.

By that time the power base in the agency had changed. My job had also been altered and I became incredibly bored and frustrated. There was some trouble over one of the accounts until eventually I was effectively and politely fired!

I was out of work for four months until I finally landed my present job as Group Account Director. I came close several times; in one case they had just hired a female and didn't want another; in another case the client would not deal with a woman. In a couple of other cases men got the jobs, but I had been judged on my merits. It was a difficult time because I was the main breadwinner of the family—my husband was in retailing and had put most of his money into the shops he was running. It was terrible to be unemployed, to suddenly have the whole burden of responsibility of supporting the family, and to not have a job.

Out of the blue a chap I used to work with offered me a job in his new sales promotion company. I also did some freelance consulting. These jobs put some bread in my mouth while I negotiated and waited for the job I have now.

The job is exactly what I want. But it has been a struggle to get there! However, I see tremendous learning and growth opportunities. All my accounts are growth accounts, I have a large chunk of the business, there are tremendous new product development opportunities and strategic opportunities, and I am being invited to go on the agency's Executive Committee.

Once I used to think that being an Account Director was like 'being way up there', similar to the idea of being a Group Account Director. Now that I have the job, I guess I will have to look at becoming Director of Client Services or Managing Director.

I hate those people who say 'I am not a woman's libber, but...' I am a woman's libber and there are no buts. I feel strongly that women do need equal opportunity and that everything should be done to promote it because they have been severely discriminated against. The woman's movement has been vital in moving things ahead. If it hadn't existed, there would have been few changes.

I have been very conscious of being an ice-breaker many times which has also given me a feeling of isolation. I have always been quite clear in my attitudes which has resulted in me being labelled a 'militant feminist'. There is that awesome responsibility that you have to succeed because if your fail they can then say, 'Look, we tried a woman and it didn't work. We won't have another one for the next five years'. I feel that I have broken the path for other women coming up the ranks. It will be a little easier for them: but everything still has a long way to go.

Myra Smith*

Aged 52, Myra is the eldest of two girls. Her father died when she was very young, and having no grandfather or uncles, she grew up without a male influence. Educated at a convent primary school and Sydney's St. George High School, she went on to Sydney University to major in mathematics, physics and statistics for a Bachelor of Science degree.

Her first job was with Bradford Cotton Mills as a trainee industrial engineer. The company was beginning to change textiles from a craft industry to a modern technological one, 'so it was a great time for graduates with technological skills'. However, she soon found that industrial engineering was not her forte ('I didn't like the meticulous approach to work where you broke everything down into its various components. Also I couldn't take the abuse from the unions'). After two years of this she was retrained in quality control at Geelong Textile College to take charge of the company's central testing laboratory. She carried out this function for six years until she had her first child.

> The laboratory work was my first experience of being in charge of other people. I got very involved in the lives of those people. I remember I had to sack a girl and I hated doing it. It wasn't the first time I had had to sack someone, but the girl's personal circumstances made it very difficult for me. I had warned her several times and finally I had to do it. I was very upset about it but fortunately I was able to help her get another job which helped me a little and her as well. When my children started to come I realised that I could no longer do both things—cope with the emotional demands of the job and the demands the children made upon me. So I went to work part-time while they were growing up.

The first part-time opportunity was at Bradmill. At first still on the technical side, she was transferred to their economic and market research area after the birth of her second daughter. One of the economists had asked for someone who understood technical processes. She entered the area as an 'adviser', but soon acquired the market research techniques.

> Once I began to think about it I realised that market research was a good thing to be in on a part-time basis. It was also the coming thing and at that stage was very heavily statistically grounded— one of my forte's from University.
>
> My next part-time job was with a leading property developer. I happened to be peeling the beans one day and saw the word 'Statistician' pop out of the rubbish paper I was putting the peelings in. The top of the ad said part-time—I couldn't believe my luck. I got the job; my boss had a wife who was a doctor and understood the problems of being a professional woman with children. He didn't care what hours I worked as long as they added up to twenty hours a week.
>
> I was there a couple of years when I became pregnant again. Because I didn't have the length of service like I had at Bradmill I thought I would have to leave. But the Managing Director said no. He had gone home to work for three months to sort out the problems of a very difficult contract involving the company. He said, 'You don't work for anyone else. Go home'. My desk and filing cabinet were shifted to my home and an office was set up. I worked for them like that for the next ten years.

Myra was also a part-time teacher in mathematics for the Higher School Certificate at the local Technical College while she was with the property developer. When her third child started school she undertook a Post-Graduate Diploma in Environmental Studies at Macquarie University.

> I decided that I needed to brighten up, to freshen up. I thought I would be the 'grannie' in the class, but I wasn't. The other students were all people who had graduated about ten to twenty years ago and had come back to learn a bit more about the world. They were nearly all science and engineering types who started out being interested in things and ended up being interested in people. I was going to convert the Diploma into a MA when I happened to read about a possibility of a scholarship at Sydney University to do a Master of Science in architecture. I applied and ended up being the Ian Buckenfeld Scholar in the Architecture School at the beginning of 1976.
>
> My thesis was on housing for the aged. By this time I was also Treasurer of the Council for the Aging and had developed a strong interest in what was happening with elderly people. At the same time I was still working part-time at both the Tech and the property

developer. I ended up over-stretching myself; I think I was working about 100 hours a week if you count the housework (I still had to do that as well). I fitted it all in because I worked from about 8 o'clock in the morning until midnight.

But I did decide to look again for a full-time job. Part-time work was very stimulating and varied, and could be done at the times that suited me. However, I had this tendency to take on more. So I reasoned that if I went back to work full-time I mightn't be tempted to take on all the little extra bits.

The first full-time job I got was as a Course Director at a Management Training College. However, the job didn't live up to its expectations; it was more like being a booking clerk for the courses. Eight months later I was successful in obtaining my present position: General Manager of the University Union. I think one of the reasons I got it was because my predecessor had been a woman—the first in this type of position in Australia. I feel she eased my way because the University was used to her being successful in the role. However, I am still the only female in the role out of all the Universities and CAEs in Australia.

The staff of the Union number 200, with twenty classified as executives—both male and female. It's a service organisation. In return for the student's union fees, we run all the support organisations in terms of the non-academic aspects of a student's life. The main one is catering—there are 26 different catering outlets spread over many buildings. We also run common rooms in all the teaching hospitals; there are half a dozen shops in which we sell stationery and other students' needs; two newsagents, and we are also very heavily into entertainment for students—big concerts, talks, all sorts of social events. We have two child-care centres, a radio station and a theatre.

I suppose I never had a career path or pattern in mind. I always looked for a job which I could enjoy. I feel that I have managed to work without neglecting my children or my husband.

I recommend part-time work because it enabled me to keep up to date. If I had left work I would never have got back in, particularly in the technological fields. I would have been considered a 'has been'. On the other hand if I had stayed at home I think I would have been an awful mother—I would have been so frustrated, something which would not have been good for the family.

I don't worry much, especially about the house. If it is in a mess it doesn't upset me. I am not fastidious or obsessive about the office either. The thing I do get stressed about is people.

When you have responsibility for other people you take on a certain amount of emotional stress. Men don't have the same feelings because they are not responsible for the family—the wife is. So they can afford to be more detached.

Just recently my eldest daughter had pneumonia which worried me terribly. At the same time one of the male managers collapsed with a stroke, aged 36, and in a way I know that the work here contributed to his condition and therefore I've contributed. I felt very bad on both fronts, and I suppose I resolved it by getting the 'flu. Perhaps that's a good out—to be able to get sick, to get the pressure off. Not to get sick: that's dangerous.

I see myself as being the umbrella who provides the climate in which other people work. I started up a personnel department here; it makes a very big difference to stability and community feeling.

I don't have any trouble in making decisions. It is the internal politics which are new to me, having to be responsible to a student Board. Most are not interested in the running of the business per se. Rather they have political motivations for being on the Board, or are heavily into the legal side so that Board meetings are run on strict parliamentary debating lines. They are people who are interested in power or politics rather than people who are interested in business.

Most have their twenty-first birthdays while on the Board. They still live at home with their parents; they haven't even earned a pay cheque let alone had to provide one. But they are all highly intelligent, young and enthusiastic and not set in their ways. They don't take obstinate stands. They are not stubborn like some business people who have always done things in a certain way and are not going to listen to anyone else. They give a good reasoned argument if they are against something.

I don't mind working with a student Board because I like dealing with people of that age. However, I don't know if I will in five years' time. While my children are around the same age I can manage.

I don't know what I will do next career-wise. In terms of a career I have probably lost about a dozen years in seniority because I did part-time work. The future looks somewhat limited, although I never can tell. My age is becoming a career obstacle.

I think women are wise to postpone the family and to get to a sufficiently high level where they can be useful. It is a strategy they should adopt. By that time they should be settled in their homes and able to afford a housekeeper. Women today have a better chance than in my day.

I don't have many people I can talk to about managerial problems and I miss that. It's lonely in the professional sense. I do meet some other professional status women because I am Deputy Chairman of the TAFE Council but they are like me: only have time for a two-minute chat and then off home for the family or other outside commitments. We are all busy people. Husbands don't see themselves as having to listen to wives' work problems; rather it is the reverse!

I wouldn't suggest that women emulate the male managerial style. I think you have to be true to yourself because it is important in a leader or a manager that people can see someone who is consistent and from whom they can expect a certain set of behaviours. Being consistent is the important thing. People have to know what they are following.

Now that there are lots of social changes for women I think they should try and get into as many jobs as possible rather than push for more changes in the legal sense. They should stop saying, 'We are discriminated against'. Get down and do it. It only needs one woman to show that something can be done and others will follow. That's what happened in this job. They knew a woman could do the job.

I also think having Queen Bees amongst women is very important. They have done all the work that is necessary and which a lot of us are not prepared to do—and I include myself in that. They have made the sacrifices, something men have never had to do.

POSTSCRIPT

All five of the women who tell their stories in this chapter have succeeded in the corporate world despite having vastly different backgrounds and experiences. Some have come from straitened circumstances, others from materially well-endowed families; some have successfully managed families and careers, others have remained single. But all had an urge, a drive to succeed, even if it was not articulated as a particular objective. Moreover, the urge survived despite various types of 'straying' from the path. These women have all faced certain conditions and survived to achieve. They are good role models for career-minded women.

The question is: do they provide sufficient inspiration to suggest that you can achieve too? Only you can answer that. However, their experiences reveal that conditions do not have to be perfect to achieve success or to become top women managers.

* Not her real name.

9

Entrepreneurial and self-employed women

ENTREPRENEURIAL AND SELF-EMPLOYED women have different problems to corporate women. Their business 'start-up' problems have been confirmed as obtaining credit, lack of business training and guidance, lack of financial planning, weak collateral position and lack of business experience (that is, competing against other businesses or in the open market place). Their general operating problems include lack of financial planning, demands of personal relationships, availability of money, reliability of employees, maintaining a favourable cash flow, organising their business operations, and hiring competent staff.[1]

Despite these difficulties (which are common to all entrepreneurs and small business operators, either male or female), women are still choosing to open their own businesses in ever increasing numbers. What has not yet become obvious is whether women entrepreneurs or small business operators can survive in business longer than their male counterparts. There is a faint suggestion that they can!

A 1986 issue of *Business Review Weekly* had this to say about self-employment among women:

> ...most women-owned enterprises are the result of women's efforts to support themselves, to bring balance and flexiblity to their lives in ways that the corporate world cannot and will not. They are out to redefine work, not to restructure the economy. What they are doing has much more to do with self-employment than enterprise.[2]

Many women who are not necessarily innovators but have marketable skills may choose self-employment. You do not need to have a million dollar idea. Self-employment gives you freedom, and also allows you to regulate your life to accommodate family, friends and career.

However, it also means taking risks, being responsible for financial matters and generally making sure that you 'keep your head above water'. It also means that you may not become the managing director of your own multi-national. Most self-employed women, including the entrepreneurs, are either solo operators or the owners of micro-businesses. Few women have developed large companies from scratch— a trait well documented amongst male entrepreneurs/proprietors. Because they have difficulties in obtaining finance, even in these more enlightened times, women-owned companies grow more slowly and have lower profits than companies owned by men.[3,4] Neither do women enter new markets with distinctly new inventions or ideas or indulge in the product innovation or modification which might lead to growth. Instead they usually remain in traditional service industries—areas in which they have either had prior experience or which require minimal start-up cash.

So self-employment and entrepreneurship offer alternatives to the 'rat-race' of the corporate world and another avenue to reach the senior levels (even if only in a small business!) How do women feel who have chosen this path? Consider the following stories—all from owner/proprietors or entrepreneurs.

Barbara Highgate*

The Managing Director of a trucking company, Barbara came to management, and to the ownership of her own business, via a circuitous route. Born in Nimbin in 1928, her parents divorced when she was young and she was reared by her grandmother. She went to school in both Nimbin and Parramatta, leaving at the age of fifteen.

Her only other formal training was a secretarial course immediately after leaving school.

She started work as a typist/secretary to the owner of a small business. This man later became Managing Director of a well known company. Barbara went with him and remained friends with him long after she married and had a son. He was to play an important role when she began her own business.

Barbara's life took an ususual turn when she good-naturedly picked up a bewildered and bedraggled couple one rainy evening at Parramatta station and helped them to find accommodation. Gem-cutters from Amsterdam, the couple had just landed in Australia and were interested in forming a business. They taught Barbara the trade and the three eventually went into business specialising in opal gem cutting. Barbara spent many years outback in the opal fields and was the first registered gem-cutter in Australia. She also developed an interest in the buying and selling of stones, realising that Australians were novices compared with the overseas professionals, who bought the opals cheaply because of the miners' lack of expertise and ignorance of market values. She tried to lobby politicians about this problem, but met with little success. Eventually she decided to quit the business. There were problems on the domestic front—her husband had become a schizophrenic, and was threatening to kill both her and her son. Action was needed. She divorced her husband and bought a trucking business. Her son was still at school, and the family had to survive. Her knowledge of trucking and the industry was zero.

Her trucking business has now been operating for fourteen years. There are only two directors, Barbara and her son, and about 40 employees. Barbara remarried but divorced her husband when he wanted to take over the business. During her time as Managing Director she has had to collect bad debts, deal with union problems, navigate the problems of the trucking industry generally, obtain suitable finance (this is where her former boss and mentor was helpful), keep her employees happy and obtain new business. She sets high standards, works extremely long hours, and is a vital force in the industry (being involved in the employers' association). Her company has no strikes, negligible labour turnover, no pilfering ('off the back of a truck'), and prides itself on being able to deliver on time. It is a successful venture, one ruled by a matriarch who is both respected and liked by her clients and employees.

However, such success has not been won without costs. Barbara relates some of her experiences and reactions:

Being upfront (i.e. the boss) is an extremely hard job. There is a lot of emotion in it, besides having to tackle everything from your bank manager to repair people, to government departments. You are trying to handle all this, your own emotions and your own style of doing business all at one and the same time. Overall, I don't know what makes a manager. I think a lot of people don't set out to do it—to be a boss. My major reason in working as hard as I do is because I like to eat and I just don't know any other way to play it. You are tied down because you must be responsible for your employees and your business. You just get into the mainstream of that and begin to channel your life that way and attempt to make a success of it.

Sometimes I've thought I would like to do something else. However, I don't think I could let the business go to someone else. Supposing the company went bad? What would happen to the people who had worked for me? The new owners would probably want to employ their own people. I wouldn't like the image or the name of the company to change either. Every-time I feel depressed I remember that and say to myself, 'Well, up and at them again', and I go on.

Perhaps the most serious problem I have had to face in this business has been the finance problem. There are not many bank managers or finance managers who believe that a woman can run a business—let alone handle money. They are extremely patronising in their attitudes. They don't believe that you are going to make it, that you will be in business for any length of time. I was fortunate to find a good loans officer in the Commonwealth Bank. We have had a good relationship over the last eight or ten years. When he comes here and says, 'How are you going, what's happening?' he knows that what we say we are going to do we will do.

It wasn't so easy in the early years of the business. I had grave problems in getting finance. Banks and companies weren't interested in touching us because they thought we wouldn't survive. I had to rely on my former boss to help me with contacts. That was the only way we were able to survive. I feel it takes many years before finance and bank people believe that you are going to make a go of it, that you will succeed.

I don't think men have the same problem because they have advantages, like old school ties. For instance, they may have even been to school with the bank manager. Women don't have those contacts. I don't know of any female bank managers or any female finance managers. You only meet males, and they are the ones guarding the barriers to getting finance. Women have to get over these barriers.

I find that if you get in a tight situation the men finance managers enjoy making you suffer. They say things like, 'We're going to block your overdraft!' The male ego comes out to show you that you are not a hot-shot businesswoman. Some of them even try the emotional side—like, 'Dear, I worry about you, I know how difficult it is for you, you are working too hard, but I have a job to do, and I have to refuse you finance'. I tell them to forget about the emotional side and just get back to the balance sheet. But the male will always try to weave this story of you being a 'poor little thing who doesn't know what she is doing'.

Another problem I have faced is on the matter of personal relationships. I have a divorce to prove that men don't relate to a woman in charge—they just want to take over. A female who has perhaps achieved in the eyes of men must be very careful in any relationship she forms. If she has her own home, cars and a company, you will often find predatory males looking for a nice safe ride. The property laws give a 50/50 split in the event of a divorce. I believe that if you owned assets before marriage you should not have to give half of them away if the marriage fails. It is only what you jointly own that should be divided.

My second husband used to ring up to make an appointment to see me. I thought it was a great joke, when I should have treated it seriously. He wanted to run the company, to take it over from me. When I heard they were bringing in this 50/50 split, I divorced him before it occurred. I would have lost the business. If the law had not changed, I would stil be married to him but I had to guard the company for my son.

My former husband hated me so much for that that he started his own business—a nice refrigerated transport business—and built it up in five years out of sheer hate. He came to see me one day and threw the balance sheet down in front of me and said, 'Look at that. Look what I've achieved'. I said, 'Goodness, you've done a great job. Would you like a cup of tea? How are you?' I just destroyed him on the spot. He saw that I didn't hate him in return and he couldn't take it.

Later he asked me to buy him out. He didn't like the business, didn't have the blood and guts to take the rough ride. In fact, he insisted I buy him out. So I did. He has now gone into another little business which means one truck, one job and he's very happy. He was on the verge of a nervous breakdown in the other business.

If he had been adult enough to understand my motivations—that is, that I would not relinquish the business even though he was my husband—none of this would have happened. But he wanted to take over, to be the boss and do my son out of his rights. I would have been happy for him to run the business, or to share management with me. I would also have liked to have had a few days off a week to get my hair done or go shopping, things like that. But give the business totally to him when he had had nothing to do with it—no way!

My first meeting with the unions was an unhappy one, although my family had had a strong union background. The Transport Workers' Union came to see me shortly after I started the business and told me that my trucks were 'black'. I said that I was quite sure I had sent them out spotlessly clean that morning. But that was not what they meant. The union informed me that none of my trucks would be unloaded at any railhead or wharf because I had failed to pay one of their members.

I replied that this particular chap still had property that belonged to me (he was supposed to have made a delivery except that the customer hadn't received the goods. The chap maintained that he had delivered the goods but couldn't remember where). The union wasn't interested in my explanation, saying that the chap had a family of six to feed and that unless I paid him I wouldn't work in the transport industry again.

I immediately had my trucks go to another depot so that they could still make deliveries to customers. We had to keep faith with the customers despite the union situation. I then rang the fellow who had caused this problem and said that I was coming out to his place to pick him up and he could take me to the spot where he had delivered the goods.

When I arrived at his house, all the lights were on (it was in the evening) and the radio was blaring. However, when I rang the door-bell the lights went out, the radio was turned off and no-one was at home.

I then organised for some people to have a look around his house when he wasn't home. They found the goods that he was supposed to have delivered stored under his house. I asked him to come into the office the next day at 11 a.m. and I paid him the money I owed him. While he was with me, one of my trucks turned up at his house and recovered the goods. I have never had any further trouble with the union or one of my employees. In fact, in the whole fourteen years I think we have lost only three drums off the trucks. Nothing has ever been stolen, which is a pretty good record.

These days I talk to a whole range of people if I have any problems. If I have a union problem I go to the union. If I have a legal problem I take it to my solicitors. But when it comes to thinking which way the business should go, and what I should do, then I just walk the floor at night. I don't sleep much—about two to three hours. The old brain just keeps going. I usually make a cup of tea and walk around trying to solve the problem. I would love to think that you could run a company in today's economic environment and be carefree, happy and enjoy life. I do get a lot of enjoyment and pride out of the business. But the heavy weight of it all is sometimes too much to bear.

Barbara's staff have a strong loyalty to her, whether they are truck drivers or office staff. Her son leaves all the major decisions to her, but will eventually run the business. Barbara is trying to improve her performance by taking short courses in subjects like public speaking. She has firm views on the ethics of business and that the customer is always right. She maintains strong standards, whether in regard to delivery to customers or treatment of employees. She is a unique individual, one who operates a profitable small business in a very volatile industry. She is a true survivor in what is in reality a male world!

Hinke Haisma

The Bulletin/Qantas Businesswoman of the Year Award winner in 1983, Hinke was born in Holland in 1948. She came to Australia with her fifteen-year-old twin sister and her mother to join two brothers who were already here. Her parents had separated. The girls were brought up on her brother's farm at Healesville, Victoria.

She matriculated at Wangaratta High in rural Victoria and went on to the Royal Melbourne Institute of Technology to qualify as an accountant. Her first job was as a junior auditor with a firm of chartered accountants. She later joined a stockbroking firm, and then, becoming interested in the mining industry, got a job with Hamersley Iron at Mount Tom Price. From there she spent two years as a purchasing officer for government stores in Alice Springs, buying for the Government Departments and the Aboriginal settlements. She also did six months' voluntary work on the Boggabilla Aboriginal Reserve on the New South Wales/Queensland border. 'I think that was a valuable experience for me because there was no money to speak of, apart from board and lodging, but it taught you to work on a voluntary basis and to work where there was a need'.

Her next career move was into computing. She had originally tried to enter this in 1971 but found 'studying computer programming language more foreign than learning English'. With money she had saved she took a year's full-time course and then joined Olivetti Australia as a programmer. She then moved into sales with the same company.

One of my tasks as a computer programmer was to develop a system for real estate agents. When I had finished it, it occurred to both my sales manager and myself that perhaps I should try and sell the system. I became so successful at this that eventually I won the 'Salesman of the Year' award, which was an around the world trip.

I also met my husband when I sold him a computer. The story there was that after many telephone calls to the company that weren't returned he became so irate that the sales manager didn't know who to send to appease him. No-one was really game to go out and see this particular gentleman, so they sent me—I was the only female sales representative. I have always believed in giving a client a total solution. It seems that on this occasion I met with immediate success because he not only bought a computer, he also became my husband. He sometimes complains that he is still paying for the after-sales service!

Hinke remained with Olivetti for about five years selling small systems to small and medium-sized businesses. However, she was aware that there was a large corporate computing world, with one to two million dollar deals, which she was not encountering. Offered the job of Marketing Manager with Olivetti (the first woman to be so), she decided against making a career in the corporate world and left to set up a contract agency for computer professionals called Parity People. The breakthrough came when she secured a one million dollar order for contract development work with a large corporation. 'We were now part of the corporate world and could grow very quickly with deals like that'. Parity People had been financed by another organisation called Parity Proprietary Limited, a small business with about four employees. Hinke was responsible for the set up of Parity People but without the financial risk, as she put it, a type of 'half-way house but still being independent'. Hinke did not work for wages, but rather a percentage of the profits she brought in. The only thing she risked was her time.

She and her husband later had the opportunity to take a controlling interest in the business but decided against it. Her husband, owner of his own business, did not know enough about the computer industry while she did not want to rely on him for finance.

Her twin sister, Nynka, who had also been working for Olivetti, left that company at the same time as Hinke and establised a shop selling second-hand Olivetti computers to the real estate industry. When the computers were superseded, the arrangement with Olivetti ended, and Nynka then set up and recruited dealers for the agency which was importing Apple Computers. After eighteen months in which she had established some 54 outlets from Geelong to Cairns she decided she wanted to become either a retailer or a distributor of computers. Hinke became involved.

I said I would give her a hand but not to involve me too much because I didn't want to go back to selling small computers. I'd done that. But after three months she had sold her first 100 Apples. In fact, she was so successful she averaged an Apple a day. She was so tired that she took off to Colorado on a skiing holiday and asked me to look after the business for a month. I didn't know anything about the Apples and was fortunate to have a thirteen-year-old boy to help me demonstrate the computers to the students and teachers who came into the shop (we were specialising in the education/school market). One month became three, and then six months, and I have never been able to get out—fortunately!

We weren't always here in Annandale. Originally when my sister wanted to become an Apple dealer she didn't have a lot of money, so my husband gave her one room in his retail business at Dulwich Hill. The paint was peeling off the walls, there were naked light bulbs and no carpet on the floor. Within one month she wanted to move from there because she felt embarrassed when people came to visit. They told her it wasn't a computer shop, it was a tyre shop, because my husband was a wholesaler in tyres and wheels for the motor industry.

One day she took the phone off the hook and went up the road and rented the first little shop that was vacant. She asked me to come over at lunch time to look at it. The shop was in Stanmore. We spent a bit of money on it and that is where we started.

We went into the education market after being at an exhibition at the Showground. Computers were arriving in the schools and we found ourselves surrounded by teachers wanting to learn about computers but not knowing where to go. The gap in the market was one of training and helping teachers and we decided to fill it. Originally, Nynka simply got in the car and went around to schools to show them how to use their computers. The business grew very quickly from there. Nowadays, we run courses in the shop at Annandale.

We are now set up in several states and have a staff of over 40. My husband has also been helping out in the business for some time. He put a General Manager into his business. But he doesn't really like our business; he thinks it is growing too fast and the pressures are very great compared to other businesses.

I am the ideas person, but Nynka can see straight away whether the idea will work. She is very much one on follow-through and making ideas work. She can stand the repetitive business, whereas I have to be getting into something new all the time.

It was a feather in our cap to become one of the seventeen dealers for IBM when they first introduced their personal computer. It was the first time that IBM had appointed dealers rather than distribute through their direct sales force. There were over 400 applications and IBM took a long time to check everyone out. We believe we were one of the smallest companies at the time to win the dealership, which meant great recognition in the industry and a credit reference!

We provide a number of unique services in this business. We have a learning centre through which we train teachers on short courses lasting from one to five days; we also have a public demand education software library of over 3000 programmes which teachers can duplicate free if they belong to the library; and we do regular newsletters to schools which have built into a 48-page magazine.

You pay a high price to run your own business, particularly in the computer industry. It is very competitive and demanding, and moves very quickly because of the technological changes. Being in a retail environment also means that the hours are long. There is so much reading to do that you really have to try and catch up on Sundays. In the last couple of years, it has been very much a seven-day-a-week job with perhaps only the odd Sunday off. If you do take a day off you pay for it the next day.

The thing I miss most is not having the time to entertain and to see friends. You have to develop friendships; friendships don't automatically happen. I try to jog for half an hour every morning and take the dog with me. That is all the time I have.

I think you can only do our type of business for a short time because it is very much in the fast lane and the strain begins to show. My sister's health is being affected and I certainly aim to slow down in the future or bring in some new partners or sell off certain sections of the business.

It is very difficult to get the right number of good people to keep up with the expansion and growth of the business. We have to grow at a minimum of 100 per cent per annum to stay in this business, because if we don't the importers open more outlets and start up more dealers. Sometimes I think we have been growing closer to 200 to 400 per cent per annum. Hence, as soon as our people learn a job and feel comfortable with it they are taken out of that comfort zone and put into new areas. There are tremendous growth paths for everyone and although this is good for your employees, if you have too much change too quickly all the time it becomes ulcer material.

I think you have fewer problems starting your own business if you are a woman. If there are some disadvantages I haven't experienced them in my business. However, in large corporate organisations you can find some disadvantages. If women are interested in going into their own business they should try and pick a gap in the market, or pick their industry or opportunity. They should also pick something they know well, and then the secret is to gather good people around you. They also have to be prepared to work very hard. They should forget about being a woman, or the fact that they may be disadvantaged, and just have a go.

However, it is very difficult to replace yourself in your own business especially if it is a small one. You can't really afford holidays because you would have to be spending lots of money on telephone calls to see how things were going. If my husband wasn't part of the business he would find it very difficult to understand why we have to work on Saturdays and Sundays because most people don't. It would be difficult for a professional man to understand a wife who was running her own business. There is less pressure on the husband if he is in a similar sized business. I think I have been very lucky. My husband understands all my business problems because he has been in his own business himself. He has been a great strength to me.

Laura Edmonds*

Aged 38 and an only child, Laura grew up in a two-woman household of mother and grandmother, her father dying when she was two. The mother was left destitute after sorting out her husband's business affairs and, being financially dependent, moved in to live with and look after her own mother. Laura was educated in Sydney at Bronte Public School and later at Randwick Girl's High. However, her mother developed cancer when she was doing the Higher School Certificate. She was immediately channelled into a secretarial career, which she didn't want to follow. Her mother was concerned for her future and wanted her to be able to earn a living and to be 'safe'.

After doing a secretarial course at Sydney Technical College one of her teachers recommended her for a job with a well known corporate raider, who was then doing a sixty million dollar business. She was seventeen.

I had also been recommended to IBM and had gone along for an interview. Even though I was very young and not very worldly I couldn't believe how plastic the organisation seemed to be. I knew that wasn't for me and ran all the way back to this other place where the books fell off the shelves when you opened the front door and everyone including the six young MBA graduates chased and beat each other to the switch when it rang. That was a very special environment and I can only say that I attribute my future career orientation to those people. They were very special.

I stayed there for six years. However, after two years I realised that I would have no expansion in status without qualifications in economics or commerce. I was the super-bored secretary until my boss began to get interested in politics and started his own political party. I asked to be transferred to that area and became assistant to the National Campaign Director and later National Liaison Officer. I had a position on the executive of the Party and was responsible for the Party's archives and press releases. The job gave me new skills and I worked very closely with the Campaign Director.

It was at this point that I decided I needed to get tertiary qualifications. I asked my boss if the firm would help me. He said, 'Yes—you can take a company car at lunch time'. So I used to get in to work at 9.30 a.m., go out at lunch time for lectures, and come back and work until midnight. I started off being a miscellaneous student because I didn't feel I could keep up the workload given the job I had with the Party.

I was eighteen months into the degree when my boss decided to get out of politics. The whole scene was shifting to Melbourne and to Don Chipp. I was asked to go down to run the administrative side of the Party. I just couldn't face living in Melbourne; I wanted to go overseas; I was nearly 25; so I thought I would opt out of politics and pursue another career direction. I left and went overseas for six months.

On my return I tried radio. I managed to get Richard Carlton who was at 2GB at the time to employ me for three hours a day. I then persuaded the Manager of Programming to give me another six hours on anything—in that way, I had a full-time job. He was going through a period of hiring and firing and he put me on. So for three hours I worked in the promotions section dealing with heavy issues and important people like Bob Hawke and for the other six I was worrying about rock and roll. At the same time I re-enrolled in my degree on a part-time basis with Macquarie (it took me another four and half years to finish it at night).

Then I struck a crisis. The management that hired me at 2GB was sacked, and I and 26 other people were also fired. All on the one day! Six months after I had begun I had no money (I had spent 8000 dollars overseas), I was living in a flat with people I didn't like, and I had no job. I was in the depths of despair and got sick. The experience made me realise that I needed to act, to have a plan and be serious about what I was doing because I had made myself too vulnerable in that organisation. I was then 26.

I was later offered a job in a small advertising agency. It was the first time in my life that I accepted a job without a brief. However, they were smart, said it was up to me to create my own situation. I ended up running the promotions company, but later asked to learn how to be an account executive in the advertising agency. I was allowed to do this, and was able to finish my degree without further distraction.

Towards the end of my degree, however, I started to branch out into philosophical areas. I became interested in the women's movement and other social issues. I then joined another small agency which was very involved in government work such as the anti-smoking campaign. We also set up the presenters for multi-cultural television. I was beginning to do things that were socially worthwhile. The only trouble was that the chap who ran the agency was an egomaniac who could never deliver. It fell to me and a couple of the others. I would be worrying about making 200 dollars on a job and he would go out and blow it all at Butler's on lunch.

I eventually drew up a manifesto on how I thought the business should be run. He agreed with everything. I was so pleased because he had agreed. But then I watched him very closely over the next few days and he once again didn't deliver. I knew he would never change, so set out to find another job.

My next step was as a researcher in industrial marketing with a small company, operated by former consultants from PA [PA Consulting]. On my second day I realised I had made a mistake in joining. I didn't like the three bosses, and the chap I had to work with was very jealous about the work. It was the first case of real discrimination that I had ever experienced. He would knock my ideas and then go off and carry them out pretending they were his. Apparently other women in the organisation had experienced similar problems. I knew I had to get out and started thinking about starting my own business.

Through friends I had some inside information about a study that was going to be done by the Department of Main Roads (DMR) into a possible second harbour crossing. I offered my services as a freelance marketing consultant/researcher. At the same time I talked to another group about being their promotions marketing consultant. I couldn't get a twelve-month contract out of either party. They just wanted me to operate on an ad hoc basis, but I wasn't prepared to go out on my own without that contract. I was also afraid of the isolation and knew I had to develop my marketing skills. After about three months of this to-ing and fro-ing, the DMR project was abandoned by the Government. I decided that I could not go out on my own under those circumstances, that the world was too undecided, that it was not formal enough for me, so I decided to look in the paper. And that's when I saw the advertisement for a public relations consultant.

The firm turned to out to be run by two women, although the

business itself was owned by a majority shareholder. After some discussions, one of the women left to pursue other interests and I joined. We are now trying to take the business from being just a public relations consultancy into the broader marketing sphere. I am now a partner in the business, and we own 35 per cent. At present we are negotiating to buy 51 per cent. The other 65 per cent is owned by an advertising agency.

At the moment I think marketing and owning my own business and building it up is my career plan. I am in a unique partnership because there is no conflict between my partner and myself. She's incredibly cooperative and honest. She understands what I am on about. I never thought I would end up with a business partner. Even though we are both strong-willed people there is a lot of room for compromise and relating to each other.

I'm still very much interested in politics—in fact my degree was in that area. At one time I worked for the Australian Labor Party during a couple of campaigns. I would like to go into politics, but I keep getting this feedback that politics is dirty, tainting, you can't be yourself, and you become compromised. I have tended to put that in the background and become interested in the women's movement instead.

I am very heavily involved with a women's management group. I got a bad deal when I came out of school because I didn't receive any career advice. My mother was in the same situation. If I have a mission in life, I think I would like to help younger women.

I want to be able to create my own destiny and I don't want it to be in the hands of anyone else. Although I live with someone, and we have an excellent relationship, I don't believe in donating your life to somebody else. I saw my mother throw her life away on me and her mother for all the wrong reasons. I am very motivated by that—by self interest, survival—so that I am not dependent on anyone, nobody has to worry about me or look after me. I am not going to be dependent on society.

Since I began my career I have learnt to be tolerant and understanding, to try and understand what motivates people, why they do certain things, why they have certain ideas. I've also learnt to get up and say what I want to and to market it—marketing has taught me that. Because I have been a secretary I have no trouble doing administrative work. The biggest shift has been taking the leap from being an administrator to being a creative person who is a thinker on issues. I think I have made the transition, but I have to watch myself so that I don't concentrate on administration.

Most people think it is easy to just carry out a task. They think the decision occurs with the people who have the ideas and that is what the premium should be on. My philosophy is that it doesn't matter how many good ideas you have if you don't have someone to carry them out it is pointless. I have positioned myself in the market-place as being not only creative but also good on backup and delivery.

One thing I don't like is the favour network. In this business you have to take 'turkeys' to lunch to get the publicity you need for your clients. I prefer selling a story on the basis of its merits. Perhaps I am being too ideological about it. I have trouble coming to grips with selling things that have to be sugar-coated.

I used to think of myself as a loner until I met my business partner. Now I see myself very much as a team person. I have had a lot of trouble lately trying to decide strategically where I'll be with offering to buy out the major partners in the business. It is a very complex arrangement because we would be actually buying our own goodwill. I have sought a lot of advice from accountants and business advisers. It is something I have never experienced before, the buying and selling of a small business. It is fascinating in terms of strategy and positioning. One piece of advice we have received is to take the clients and just walk out and go our own way: but that's not ethical. Both my partner and I feel strongly about that. It seems a hard and nasty way of doing business: we want to negotiate a more reasonable settlement to everyone's advantage. It comes back to the old situation: we don't want to be in a lose/lose or a win/lose position. We want a win/win situation where all the parties walk away feeling as if they have achieved something. I guess we come right back to the way men and women do business!

Laura is currently involved in another crisis. Her male domestic partner is embarking on the mid-life career crisis and this is causing some tensions in the relationship. Laura is also now earning considerably more than he which is causing other strains. Her career appears to be increasingly successful, while his is entering a plateau phase. His self-confidence is ebbing away, while hers is growing. Moreover, she is now entering her late thirties and has to decide whether to have a child before it is too late. While her professional career is in its ascendancy, her domestic life is entering a troubled zone. Her mother is also shortly to retire and will be financially dependent on her. New decisions or directions have to be taken. It is the constant dilemma of the career woman, either corporate or independent. Careers are not always necessarily straightforward because account has to be taken of life stages. Laura appears to be facing such a situation. (Her original employer, the corporate raider, taught her how to approach such matters).

He was an alternative; an enigma in the business community. He was successful by going in the other door and he showed me how to do it. He was so alternative that I would sit there each day and watch what he was doing because it was so extraordinary. He just debunked the myth that everything was hard.

Rachael Goldstein*

Aged 47, Rachael was born in Brisbane but grew up in Melbourne. She is the eldest of two girls. Her father was a doctor who later became a cancer specialist. Her mother did not work outside the home. Rachael was educated at a Church of England Grammar School before going on to university to complete an arts degree. While there she did some casual work in a public relations agency which prompted her to apply for jobs in the industry on gaining her degree. She obtained a job after writing a report on the Australian fashion industry and worked in the fashion public relations arena until she was 24. Apart from the public relations agency she spent a couple of years with a textile house, and several years with a women's hair products company. She knew a lot about fashion but little about business.

She then became Advertising and Promotions Manager for a well known hotel group in Melbourne. A glamorous life began, mixing with cabaret artists, visiting dignitaries and arranging publicity. During this time she also married the Director of Sales of a rival hotel chain. Marriage interrupted the career, because her husband didn't want her to work.

> During the three years we were married I fiddled around with frivolous things. I used to go to the hairdresser twice a week and I had a little boutique for a while. I made quite a few television commercials and did a bit of photographic modelling, which was all terribly 'thing' with false eyelashes, etc. I also did a lot of overseas travelling with my husband. I had never been outside the country and thought it was great going first class around the world, staying at all the best hotels. But then I suddenly became bored. He wouldn't let me work, he didn't want me to study and I didn't particularly feel like having children. I didn't know what I was doing there. Something snapped in me one day, and I walked out of the marriage.

Unfortunately, she had dropped most of her public relations contacts while she was married. Her father had always opposed her interest in this industry, believing it to be not a 'nice thing for a young lady to do'. So she looked around and entered the Victorian education system (at that time they hired people with only a degree as teachers). She taught for four days a week while attending teacher's college on the other day to acquire a Teaching Certificate. This lasted for three years until she again changed direction, obtaining a job with an advertising agency.

> The more I got to deal with big companies and their marketing people the more I realised I knew little about business. In all my career I had never had to worry about profitability or budgeting or anything that was really central to the business arena. I began to understand that I had to develop a career, that life was real, that I would probably be working all my life and at some stage a woman becomes superfluous if she doesn't have some really heavy skills to offer.
>
> I then saw an advertisement for a product manager with a large multi-national marketing company. I took the opportunity, although it meant moving away from Melbourne, because I felt I would never get another chance like this—I didn't have a Bachelor of Commerce or other skills like that. I became heavily involved, and they sent me on several marketing courses including an international one. However, after four years I began to realise that I would be 'wedded' to the company, so began to look around.

A conversation with a headhunter resulted in Rachael becoming the interstate manager of one of his offices. She thought she was entering a partnership, but this did not transpire. Nevertheless, she took the position because it gave her experience in managing an office and people. She did this for eighteen months before starting her own personnel consultancy on a shared office basis, using another company's registered name. However, because of the lack of back-up she went out on her own six months later.

> I finally realised that I would have to put my own name up front and go for broke. Somewhere underneath I had always thought I would have my own business. I saw it as a way of doing my own thing, and it drew together all the things I had been doing. I had also realised when I was moving into my late thirties that I didn't know of many women who were in senior executive positions in corporations. This was of course in 1976. So the only way I could really have independence, determine my own life and do what I wanted to do was through my own business.
>
> I am in a very competitive business, and because of this I have to keep a fairly high profile. Contacts are extremely important. We are in the upper end of the personnel business concentrating on the total range of the marketing mix. We have link-ups with other companies both interstate and overseas.
>
> As a woman I am competing mostly against male-oriented and male-led concerns. An old boys' network operates in that

environment. You have people who have worked together, played sport together, or drink together. It is difficult to compete against that.

As the owner of your own business you have to think completely differently to when you just worked for a pay packet. I have to think about cash flows, bank managers, overdrafts, and whether the business is up or down. I also have to motivate my own staff. This is a very tough business and we always have to be mindful of the fact that we might be running hot one minute but down the next. We also have to deal with people who may change their minds—both firms and individuals. You can do all the wonderful things to find the right person for the job and have no result.

Because I haven't had any formal training in operating a business, I have had to learn by doing and making mistakes. The 1982 to 1983 recession was a fairly salutory lesson as well because I had to cut back on staff to make sure I survived. A lot of people, including myself, didn't see the recession coming, and it is possibly the same with the next one. But you are somewhat at the mercy of outside influences in running a business. There are lots of things you would like to do, but if the economy is going up and down it makes it difficult to plot a course. I have a strategic plan, which was expansionary, but am in the process of cutting back on staff again because of the economic situation. Despite your plan, you have to be pragmatic, you have to pull back and say, 'Sorry, we will think about that next year'.

One of the mistakes I have made is to install an unsatisfactory computer system. I was given advice from one of our group companies, but hesitated for about two years. Finally, I talked to other people, the business was becoming more complicated, my competitors were going that way, and I needed a good system. The computers we chose were a mistake, not nearly powerful enough for our needs. I have had to scrap the whole system and start again.

Another thing I have learned is that women don't get an equal go at jobs when we try to place them. I know it is illegal now, but the companies still get around it. When they are briefing us they say things like: 'This is an automative account, which is a male environment, so we really need someone who is going to talk the language of the dealers and go out and get drunk with them because they are a pretty rough lot'. I tell them that it is illegal and we will submit both male and female candidates. But you know darn well that the woman won't get the job and there is nothing you can do about it. There are a number of very chauvinistic people out there in the business community who still think women are lightweight. I wouldn't be surprised if they thought the same about an all-female consultancy like mine.

I have employed men in the past but find in this business that women have better empathy with people. Men go through the motions and do all the right things in meeting the brief, but a good female has something extra over a male. I know there are a lot of successful men in the industry. Perhaps it is the men I have selected. It is very difficult to get the right type of people to work for you.

I would sometimes like a partner because I find it hard to get away on holidays or to be sick. I may have to bring one in because the load sometimes is really significant. Many people in this type of business do have partners.

I have been trying to minimise my involvement in day-to-day operations, like interviewing, so that I can concentrate on developing new business and administration. But with my recent cut-backs I have had to change that approach. If you don't have productive consultants you have to come back in and do it yourself. Maybe that is bad management, but I find that the consultants at the end of the day go home at 5.30 and that is that. With me, the work keeps continuing because I have to ensure that the business survives. Everyone just sees the owner of a business making megabucks and lying around enjoying themselves, which in my case is just not true. I had no concept of what running a business would be like, or how hard it is, when I was working for someone else. I think it is very hard.

Dr Alessandra Pucci

Voted the 1985 *The Bulletin*/Qantas Businesswoman of the Year, Dr Pucci was born in 1942 in Ethiopia of Italian parents. She lived there until she finished school, then went to Italy to undertake undergraduate studies at the University of Pisa. She followed this with graduate studies in pharmaceutical chemistry (University of Pisa) and biomedical science (University of Florence). She came to Australia in 1970 together with her husband and son. Completing a Doctor of Philosophy in immunology through the Sydney University Medical School, she worked there for about seven years doing medical research. She set up her own business in 1981 after thinking about it for two years. She is the founder and managing director of Australian Monoclonal Development Proprietary Limited, one of the first companies in the world to have turned the theoretical promise of complex new ideas in biotechnology into the reality of a marketable product.

The research career was going fine, I was publishing, but it didn't have too many practical satisfactions. I was beginning to see new biotechnology companies being set up in the United States. This represented a very exciting new development and I thought I should enter the field. The technological area I was working in presented exploitable opportunities in terms of the commercial world.

Some finance came through my family, but most of the initial finance came privately through friends and groups that I organised myself. Later on I was able to obtain an Industrial Development Incentive Grant from the Government. It was a very substantial project grant and very, very crucial to the development of our expertise and the new products. The grant enabled us to carry out the research and development which I thought necessary because the technology at the time was more basic science than industrial technology. We thus had to do a lot of work, and employ a lot of resources, to transform it from a university research commodity into a technological tool.

I started out with partners. My first two partners were my husband and a friend who provided some of the finance. We also gave some equity to the ten staff who started with us in the company. The senior scientist came from England because that is where the actual technology originated. During the period of the research and development grant we had eighteen people working for us (the laboratory was opened in 1982). Once we had developed some industrial technology we had to proceed to produce actual products. We then went to several corporate organisations, including the management investment companies (MICs), which had been set up by the Government to give incentive to companies when they were still at the level of growth where they needed finance.

We obtained some finance from one of the MICs. That brought with it a requirement for a more formalised board. So where once we were three partners, we now had a representative of the MIC and a chairman. The two additional people brought in a lot of management experience. The chairman is an external chairman but is very active and contributes a lot to the company. Our number of employees has also expanded to over 30.

I think my scientific background has helped me in management because you have a certain approach and attitude to problems and problem solving. It is quite an exact one, in fact more exact than the approach adopted by the usual manager. It became clear to me very early that I was capable of analysing issues and then taking decisions very quickly when they were needed. I did have to learn the details of running the business. However, it was easy to some extent because we have a research and development company which isn't much different from manging a research project like I was doing before.

Obviously I had to look at some other aspects, like managing people. I don't think I have completely covered that because I am dealing with senior scientists who are very independent types of people. They regard themselves as being untouchable and are prima donnas in their own right. I didn't entirely solve it until I gave the job to someone else. I now have a full-time research director who looks after the day to day contact with the other scientists. However, I still keep very much in touch through weekly meetings to discuss problems and progress on projects.

My husband is in charge of production and we discuss things almost 24 hours a day. I have learnt a great deal from him. I keep a tight grip on the financial side. While I have taken advice from accountants and other advisers, I have a better idea of forecasting than some of the more experienced management investment advisers who base their budgeting on probability methods. I find that very artificial, so I keep a watchful eye on expenses and am very meticulous in implementing budgets. The economics, planning and actual implementation of budgets has been one of my strong points. I think my analytical background in science has helped here.

I am the Managing Director and Chief Executive Officer of the company and have a total of six people reporting to me. Worldwide there are very few women in biotechnology. I think my role has been viewed in the past with a 'watch and see attitude'. The fact that we have had certain successes and that the company is working and making progress—developing products and getting contracts—and above all has a good reputation, means that my position is now being accepted. It obviously works so that people now think that there is nothing wrong with a woman being a chief executive officer.

One of the problems with biotechnology companies is that they grow too fast. I am taking a very cautious approach: I want to build a strong position first here in New South Wales and then elsewhere. However, we already export around the world and have a worldwide distributor network.

Winning the Businesswoman of the Year Award was a great thing in terms of recognition of the work being done by the company. The publicity the company received was tremendous. It brought our activities and this new area into the limelight; they were less well known before.

Personally, I have had many opportunities to talk to people, present papers, or just talk about the company. The Award has meant that I have received a lot of publicity and have been able to talk about science to a wider audience. I have enjoyed the Award and the benefits it has brought.

I travel pretty extensively interstate because I am on the Australian Industrial Research and Development Incentive Board, the Australian Plastic and Chemical Industry Council and the New South Wales Science and Technology Council.

Being in my own business I have been able to implement and, to some extent, experiment with new ways of management, new techniques and new approaches. There is little risk involved because I am able to control it. If I was working for a corporation I don't think I would have had the same freedom to implement my ideas. I am quite positive I would have encountered a lot of opposition because a number of things I do are outside the general bounds of conventional management. For instance, I don't have time for the conventional ways of budgeting and accounting. Obviously there are a number of accountants in the company who do the conventional thing. I don't follow those methods as my Bible at all. That is one thing that would have obviously raised a few eyebrows.

I have a vision of where I want the company to go. We have a very well-defined short-term corporate strategy as well as longer-term objectives. I try to keep the options open for the long run.

My strong scientific background has deterred people from making fun of my technical competency. But there have been doubts about my other skills—such as in management, in accounting and the various aspects of the business where I didn't have any formal qualifications. That is where people mostly had reservations. Fortunately those reservations are covered now. But I didn't encounter any doubts in the context of technology, which was important for the business, seeing that it is centred on technology.

I have very distinct negative feelings towards the total masculine attitude to management—the attitude of total control, dominance, takeovers—and its activity. On the other hand I dislike equally the feminine type of management which fears making decisions, fears consequences of actions and has a petty attitude. I try to adopt a more neutral, genderless, management style. I find I watch for the 'masculine tinge' in my advisers. I heartily dislike the masculine negativity of things, that instinct to kill, or that aggressiveness that is in management. Whenever I have taken that away, there has always been a very positive result professionally. People can be confident and assertive and not weak. But the component that is excessive is the killer instinct—that is definitely unnecessary. It doesn't add anything to how you operate as a manager.

I try to appear competent in whatever I do. That is my main concern. The other is not to become emotional. This is something I have to guard against with some care. From time to time I do lose my cool. However, I have improved with maturity. My outbursts are usually when there is an overload of too many things and then there is an explosion. But I find that is very negative and I definitely believe that letting it all out does not help at all. It especially doesn't help relationships in the office. It is something I have had problems with in the past.

I am quite fortunate because I have an understanding family. My son and husband take a lot of pressure off me; they are more humorous than I and can add a touch of humanity to the family. I find it quite difficult to unwind, particularly when I go home and have to do the things that are required of a good wife and mother. I think I have a lack there somehow. I have a housekeeper to look after the house. I almost don't do anything in that area.

I admire women in management. They have a commitment which is also a moral one. Women managers are much more ethical than the men that I've met and I believe it goes back to this commitment—or cause—or their belief in the company. Women nuture the creator, or company; they have a protective instinct towards it. Men milk the creator rather than nurture. Women have a sense of destiny which goes beyond the self-interest of men.

However, I dislike women's aggressiveness in management. I also dislike the fact that some women are quite chatty and petty and run their businesses as if they were with their friends. Some women are too frivolous for business. Others mix personal with professional relationships; they cannot divorce the two.

My advice to other women is to first of all become competent in an aspect of business, not management itself immediately. Management is an ability that is built up over the years and is to some extent specific to the business. Women should understand the business they are in in its various aspects, whether financial, technical or other. They must not go into a business they don't understand. You really have to prepare yourself very well. Then they should look around to surround themselves with supportive, rather than antagonistic, people. A lot of women are supportive. You must build up a buffer around yourself because you are going to need one. Finally, adopt a nuturing approach to the business rather than a milking approach; take the protective rather than the killer type of attitude and generally be ethical in business. That way you can succeed as a woman in management and in your own business.

POSTSCRIPT

The above evidence should convince you that women can be successful as businesswomen. Despite various doubts and fears, success has been achieved by them either as solo operators, partners, managing directors or chief executive officers. Women mostly succeed in service areas as our case studies reveal. However, Dr Pucci does not conform to that norm: she is an entrepreneur, an innovator. She has entered new markets with distinctly new products and is on a marked growth curve. In fact, international expansion is a probable long-term objective for her company. She is a 'woman of enterprise' and a role model in a technological and exciting area.

So you can achieve success by being either an organisational manager or a woman of enterprise or by being independently employed. The choice is yours.

* Not her real name.

10

Taking off the blinkers

IF YOU THOUGHT you could never succeed in reaching senior management or being your own boss, now is the time to reconsider. Sufficient women have gone before you to prove that it can be done. Few have been superwomen. In fact some have had few of the ordinary advantages of life in the early stages of their careers. Yet they persevered, and they *succeeded*!

If you have not yet made any steps in this direction, it is time you took your blinkers off and reassessed your situation, skills and motivations *and started to think in terms of a career.*

If you are part of the way there, struggling to maintain your grip on the ladder and having second thoughts about whether you have taken the right track, *re-read the stories in our case studies and take fresh heart.* Each of those women has had her doubts (in fact some still do—it is only natural), yet each has continued in spite of frustrations and adversity.

Women often argue that there are not sufficient role models for them to emulate. Our examples suggest that such role models do exist, in all walks of life. What are the qualities that earmark these women from the ordinary?

The evidence suggests the following:

- Successful women have a career direction or an urge to succeed in some way or other—some want to be famous, others to be appreciated, some want to acquire money, while others wish to avoid 'just being a typist'.

- Successful women have had either some support from their families, or if lacking through being one of a large family, from mentors or advisers at various stages. The important thing is that most have had support in some form or other when they most needed it.

- Successful women have all had 'dormant' periods in their careers, or pre-careers, before the direction became clear. Sometimes the plateau stage was short; in others a longer period of time eventuated while families were raised and husbands supported. All have had an 'awakening'—and the challenge has been to realise their potential.

- Successful women have all followed through on projects, jobs, contacts, until their competencies were proven. Where skills were lacking they acquired new knowledge by either undertaking courses, accepting advice, or just learning from their own and others' experience. Being prepared to learn was a keynote in their success.

- Successful women have undertaken the unpleasant tasks of management because they have to be done. Few run away from their responsibilities even though the actions required may conflict with personal value systems or they may not be considered 'nice'.

- Successful women have also tried to introduce more compassionate styles of management rather than slavishly follow the tried and trusted male managerial model. Some have had firm ideas on how management should be conducted; others have been less vehement. However, most have recognised the difficulties involved in handling people and have taken appropriate action to either improve their own styles or to employ someone else in the management mode.

- Successful women have usually known their businesses thoroughly. There are no 'dilettantes' among them. They are *professionals.*

- Successful women have faced prejudice, stereotypical reactions and discrimination and managed to cope with it. While they are all acutely aware of being a woman in a man's world, not one holds any bitterness about prejudiced treatment they may have received. Instead, they have been too busy undertaking new jobs, enterprises, courses, projects—in fact, too busy *achieving.*

- Successful women have also tried to have 'normal' female lives in the sense of marriage or defacto relationships, and children. Although not always successful in relationships, they have a sense of balance in their lives.

- Successful women, despite their doubts and fears, have all become *managers and enterprising people.* They are not 'female' this or 'female' that. They have transgressed the boundaries that others say hold them back.

Given these characteristics of successful women, what, then, are the characteristics of unsuccessful women—those women who say they wish to go far in their careers but in fact never do? Consider the following:

- Unsuccessful women lack drive or incentive to achieve. They expect life to 'happen' to them and bemoan their fate when others pass them by. They sit and brood about how 'lucky' everyone else is and how they 'never had a chance'.

- Unsuccessful women refuse to undertake new courses or listen to advice because they don't have time or no-one understands their problems. If someone was interested in them they could remedy all of it. They need constant reassurance and support and expect to be 'forgiven' if they make mistakes or things don't work out as expected.

- Unsuccessful women expect results in a very short time—they are not prepared to sit out the sometimes long years before success becomes evident. They want others to smooth their way, think others have it 'easy', that they are 'as good as them', but can't understand why they never have the same level of success.

- Unsuccessful women try to take short cuts by copying the success of others but fail to recognise the hard work that goes on behind the scenes or the uniqueness of the original achiever. They try to use 'contacts', their success with men, and other such methods to leapfrog ahead. They do not realise that they do not have the persistence to follow through and achieve in their own right. They usually show this quite soon if they have managed to masquerade their way up the ladder.

- Unsuccessful women become 'hung-up' over the 'discriminatory' treatment they receive from 'everybody'. They demand equality and make scenes in meetings to loudly assert their 'rights'.

- Unsuccessful women are 'scatty' in their business dealings and relationships and think this is being 'feminine'. They go into business or occupations which are 'nice', 'safe' and 'where I can be liked'. They get involved in social issues to the exclusion of all else. They think 'making money' is 'offensive'.

- Unsuccessful women are fearful of taking the first step, of committing themselves, of failing, of 'having a go'—but they also want the money, the perks, the glamour and the excitement of a career.

THE LAST WORD

As we said in the first chapter, success is not easily won. But trying can be stimulating, interesting, rewarding—and *fun*. Women have much to contribute in management, either in the organisational sense or as independent operators. More should be in management, and more should be at the senior levels. Why? Because each woman is unique, as Edith Highman puts it:

> To each one is given a marble to carve for the wall;
> A stone that is needed to heighten the beauty of all;
> And only her soul has the magic to give it grace;
> And only her hands have the cunning to put it in place;
> Yet, the task that is given to each one, no other can do;
> So the errand is waiting; it has waited through ages for you;
> And now you appear; and the hushed ones are turning their gaze;
> To see what you do with your chance in the chamber of days. [1]

rofile updates

Following are the current (late 1987) situations of the women whose histories were described in chapters 8 and 9:

Laura Edmonds is now Managing Director of a public relations agency which is an off-shoot of a well-known Australian advertising agency.
Rachael Goldstein has just taken two partners into her business and moved premises.
Hinke Haisma has sold 67% of the business and is now involved in developing innovative marketing ventures. She still retains 33% of the original business.
Barbara Highgate is still in the same position, but has moved her business premises.
Emily Johnson has recently changed advertising agencies.
Helen Marshall has achieved her ambition of becoming Publisher.
Joan Playford has recently received a promotion to General Manager level.
Dr Alessandra Pucci is still in the same business.
Myra Smith is still in the same position.
Jane Thompson is still in the same position.

Notes

Chapter 1

1   Harragan, B.L. (1983) 'Women and Men at Work: Jockeying for Position' in (ed.) *Jennie Farley: The Woman in Management: Career and Family Issues* ILR Press: New York State School of Industrial and Labor Relations, Cornell University, pp. 12–19

Chapter 2

1   Neary, J. (1985) *The Decade—Is That All there Is? Women and Employment—Issues for the Future* Address to United Nations Association of Australian National Status of Women Committee Conference: 'That Was the Decade for Women—What Next', Melbourne, 20–22 September

2   Still, L.V. (1986a) 'Women in Management: The Case of Australian Business' *Human Resource Management Australia, 24,* 1 (Feb), pp. 32–37

3   *Ibid*

4   Still, L.V. (1986b) 'Women Managers in Advertising: An Exploratory Study' *Media Information Australia, 40,* May, pp. 24–30

5   Office of Women's Affairs, Victoria (1981) *Women in Management: A Survey with Comparisons* Department of the Premier

6   Taperell, K., C. Fox and M. Roberts (1975) *Sexism in Public Service: The*

Employment of Women in Australian Government Administration Royal Commission on Australian Government Administration, Discussion Paper No. 3, Canberra: Australian Government Publishing Service

7 Carter, M., K. Tarlo and J. Trevithick (1980) *Career Patterns of Women in the Australian Public Service* Planning and Statistical Services Section, Planning Research and Information Branch, Canberra: Public Service Board

8 Carter, M., G. Rothman and P. Thorne (1982) *Women in the Australian Public Service—Distribution and Career Patterns* Public Service Board Research Paper 4, Australian Government Publishing Service: Office of the Public Service Board

9 Review of New South Wales Government Administration (1977) *Directions for Change, An Interim Report*, (Professor P. Wilenski, Commissioner), November

10 Equal Employment Opportunity Unit (1983) *Women in the Public Service of Victoria: A Discussion Paper* Public Service Board of Victoria, August

11 Committee on the Status of Women Academics, FAUSA (1977) *Survey on Women in Australian Universities and Report on Characteristics of Academic Job Applicants* Federation of Australian University Staff Associations, November

12 Cass, B., M. Dawson, D. Temple, S. Will, and A. Winkler (1983) *Why So Few? Women Academics in Australian Universities* Sydney University Press

13 Sawer, M. (1984) *Towards Equal Opportunity—Women and Employment at the Australian National University* Report of the Working Party of the Association of Women Employees, Canberra: Australian National University

14 Poiner, G. (1984) 'Changing Opportunities for Women in Universities: A Question of Responsibility and Will', pp. 26–34, in (ed.) *Shirley Randell: The Way Forward: Women in Higher Education Management in Australia* Report of a National Conference, 18–20 July, 1984, Armidale, The Australian College of Education, June 1985

15 Mathews, J. (1982) 'The Changing Profile of Women in the Law' *The Australian Law Journal, 56* December, pp. 634–642

16 Equal Opportunity Board, Victoria (1983) *Women in Chartered Accounting* The Board, August

17 Sampson, S. (1986) 'Promotion in Government Schools' *Education News, 19,* 7 (March), pp. 38–41, 47

18 Brown, T. and C. Turner (1985) *Women, Men and their Careers: Gender Domains in the Female Profession of Social Work* Paper presented in the Women's Studies Section, ANZAAS Festival of Science, Monash University, August

19 Williams, C. (1985) 'Gender Aspects of Flight Attending as an Occupation in Australia' Paper presented to SAANZ Conference, University of Queensland, August

20 Byrne, E.M. (1985) *Women and Engineering: A Comparative View of New Initiatives* Bureau of Labour Market Research Monograph Series No. 11, Canberra: AGPS, p. 130

21 Sams, D. (1982) 'Occupational and Industrial Segregation of Female Employment in Australia: A Review' in (ed.) *Women in the Labour Force:*

The Proceedings of a Conference, 12–13 August Bureau of Labour Market Research Monograph Series No. 4, Canberra: AGPS, 1984, pp. 66–92

22 Women's Bureau (1984) *Women and Labour Market Programs: Submission to the Committee of Inquiry into Labour Market Programs* Department of Employment and Industrial Relations, Canberra, August

23 Giles, P. (1985) *Women Workers and Technology Bargaining: 'The Light Just Keeps on Flashing'*, Contributed Paper No. 2, Women's Bureau, Department of Employment and Industrial Relations, Canberra: AGPS

24 Still, L.V. (1986a) *op cit*

25 Women's Bureau (1983) *Gender Wage Differentials in Australia* Information Paper No. 1, Department of Employment and Industrial Relations, Canberra, August

26 Hearn, J. (1982) 'Notes on Patriarchy, Professionalization and the Semi-Professions' *Sociology, 16*, 2 (May), pp. 184–202

27 Grieve, N. and M. Perdices (1981) 'Patriarchy: A Refuge from Maternal Power? Dinnerstein's Answer to Freud' in *Australian Women: Feminist Perspectives* Melbourne: Oxford University Press

28 Brown and Turner (1985) *op cit*

29 Sampson (1986) *op cit*

Chapter 3

1 Davies, B. (1985) 'Attitudinal Barriers to the Participation of Women in Higher Educational Management' in (ed.) *Shirley Randell: The Way Forward: Women in Higher Education Management in Australia* Report of a National Conference 18–20 July, 1984, Armidale, The Australian College of Education, June, pp. 44–57

2 Winkler, A. (1983) 'Feminism or Female Rejection: Sex-Role Attitudes of Academic Women and Men' in B. Cass et al. *Why So Few? Women Academics in Australian Universities* Sydney University Press, pp. 176–195

3 Review of New South Wales Government Administration (1977) *Directions for Change: An Interim Report* prepared by Professor Peter Wilenski, Commissioner, Review, November

4 Women's Bureau (1984) *Women and Labour Market Programs: Submission to the Committee of Inquiry into Labour Market Programs* Department of Employment and Industrial Relations, August

5 Broverman, J.K., S.R. Vogel, D.M. Broverman, R.E. Clarkson and P.S. Rosenkrantz (1972) 'Sex Role Stereotypes: A Current Appraisal' *Journal of Social Issues, 28*, 2, pp. 59–78

6 McGregor, D. (1967) *The Professional Manager* New York: McGraw-Hill, p. 23

7 Schein, V.E. (1975) 'Relationship between Sex Role Stereotypes and Requisite Management Characteristics among Female Managers' *Journal of Applied Psychology, 60*, 3 (June), pp. 340–344

8 Steinberg, R. and S. Shapiro (1982) 'Sex Differences in Personality Traits of Female and Male Master of Business Administration Students' *Journal of Applied Psychology, 67*, 3, pp. 306–310

9 Reif, W.E., J.W. Newstrom, and R.M. Monczka (1975) 'Exploding Some

Myths About Women Managers' *California Management Review, 17,* 4, pp. 72–79

10 Golembiewski, R. (1977) 'Testing Some Stereotypes About the Sexes in Organisations: Differential Satisfaction with Work?' *Human Resource Management, 16,* 4 (Winter), pp. 21–24

11 Dipboyne, R.L. (1978) 'Women as Managers—Stereotypes and Realities' in (ed.) B.A. Stead *Women in Management* Englewood Cliffs, N.J.: Prentice-Hall, pp. 2–9

12 Courtenay, B. (1986) 'Time to Slot More Women into Top Positions' *The Financial Australian* Monday, 29 September, p. 17

13 Terborg, J.R. and M.D. Zalesny (1980) Women as Managers: A Review of Research on Occupational Sex Discrimination, in (eds.) K.M. Rowland, M. London, G.R. Ferris and J.L. Sherman *Current Issues in Personnel Management,* Boston: Allyn and Bacon Inc, pp. 357–366

14 Still, L.V. (1986a) 'Women in Management: The Case of Australian Business' *Human Resource Management Australia, 24,* 1 (Feb), pp. 32–37

15 Still, L.V. (1986b) 'Women Managers in Advertising: An Exploratory Study' *Media Information Australia, 40,* May, pp. 24–30

16 Terborg, J.R. and D.R. Ilgen (1975) 'A Theoretical Approach to Sex Discrimination in Traditionally Male Occupations' *Organisational Behavior and Human Performance, 13,* pp. 352–376

17 Donnell, S.M. and J. Hall (1980) 'Men and Women as Managers: A Significant Case of No Significant Difference' *Organisational Dynamics, 8,* 4, pp. 60–77

18 Ruble, T.L. (1983) 'Sex Stereotypes: Issues of Change in the 1970s' *Sex Roles, 9,* 3 (March), pp. 397–402

19 Dubno, P. (1985) 'Attitudes Towards Women Executives: A Longitudinal Approach' *Academy of Management Journal, 28,* 1, pp. 235–239

20 *Ibid*

21 Terborg, J.R., L.H. Peters, D.R. Ilgen, and F. Smith (1977) 'Organisational and Personal Correlates of Attitudes Towards Women as Managers' *Academy of Management Journal, 20,* pp. 39–100

22 Stevens, G.E. and A.S. DeNisi (1980) 'Women as Managers: Attitudes and Attributions for Performance by Men and Women' *Academy of Management Journal, 23,* 2, pp. 355–360

23 Cromie, S. (1981) 'Women as Managers in Northern Ireland' *Journal of Occupational Psychology, 54,* 2 (June) pp. 87–91

24 Dubno (1985), *op cit*

25 Terborg et al. (1977), *op cit*

26 Partington, G. (1986) 'Standards Fall As Women Kick At Seats of Learning' *The Bulletin,* 9 September, pp. 49–54

27 McCully, M.R. (1986) Letter to the Editor *The Bulletin,* 23 September, p. 19

28 Courteney, B. (1986) 'Time To Slot More Women into the Top Positions' *The Financial Australian,* 29 September, p. 17

29 Kanter, R.M. (1977) *Men and Women of the Corporation* New York: Basic Books

30 Bartol, K.M. (1980) 'Female Managers and Quality of Working Life: The Impact of Sex-Role Stereotypes' *Journal of Occupational Behaviour, 1,* 3 (July), pp. 205–221

31 Still, L.V. (1986a) *op cit*
32 Still, L.V. (1986b) *op cit*
33 Business Council of Australia (1986) *Equal Opportunity for Women: The Corporate Experience* The Council, Foreword by the President, R.J. White, AO
34 Working Party on Affirmative Action Legislation (1985) *Report of the Party* Canberra: AGPS, September, p. 25

Chapter 4
1   Peters, T.J. and R.J. Waterman, Jr. (1982) *In Search of Excellence: Lessons from America's Best-Run Companies*, New York: Harper and Row
2   Blanchard, K. and S. Johnson (1984) *The One Minute Manager*, Fontana/ Collins
3   Iococca, L. with W. Novak (1984) *Iococca: An Autobiography*, New York: Bantum Books
4   Hertz, L. (1986) *The Business Amazons: Women Entrepreneurs* London: Andre Deutsch
5   Christie, M. (1986) *Targeting Success: From a Woman's Point of View* William Heinemann Australia
6   Cardwell, L. (1985) 'Managing Women—A Man's View' *Women in Management Review*, *1*, 3 (Autumn), pp. 158–161
7   Still, L.V., J.J. Ray, and C. Guerin (1986) *Assertiveness and Women Managers* Working Paper, Women in Management Series, Paper No. 10, School of Business, Nepean College of Advanced Education
8   Sargent, A.C. (1983) *The Androgynous Manager* New York: AMACOM
9   Maccoby, M. (1976) *The Gamesman: The New Corporate Leaders* New York: Simon and Schuster, p. 244
10 Motowidlo, S.J. (1982) 'Sex-role Orientation and Behavior in a Work Setting' *Journal of Personality and Social Psychology, 42*, 5 (May), pp. 935–945
11 Lee, A.G. and V.L. Scheurer (1983) 'Psychological Androgyny and Aspects of Self-Image in Women and Men' *Sex Roles 9*, 3 (March), pp. 289–306
12 McPherson, K.S. and S.K. Spetrino (1983) 'Androgyny and Sex-Typing: Difference in Beliefs Regarding Gender Polarity in Ratings of Ideal Men and Women' *Sex Roles, 9*, 4 (April), pp. 441–451
13 Mayes, S.S. (1979) 'Women in Positions of Authority: A Case Study of Changing Sex Roles' *Signs: Journal of Women in Culture and Society, 4*, 3 (Spring), pp. 556–568
14 Powell, G.N. (1982) Sex-role Identity and Sex: An Important Distinction for Research on Women in Management, *Basic and Applied Social Psychology, 3*, 1 (March), pp. 67–79
15 Eisenstein, H. (1984) *Contemporary Feminist Thought* London: George Allen and Unwin, p. 63
16 *Ibid*
17 Pedler, M. and R. Fritchie (1985) Training Men to Work With Women, *Women in Management Review, 1*, 2 (Summer), pp. 75–84
18 Eisenstein, H. *op cit*, p. 66

19   Kanter, R.M. (1977) *Men and Women of the Corporation* New York: Basic Books

Chapter 5

1   Westbrook, M.T. and L.A. Nordholm (1984) 'Characteristics of Women Health Professionals with Vertical, Lateral and Stationary Career Plans' *Sex Roles, 10,* No. 9–10 (May), pp. 743–756

2   Little, J.E. (1985) *The Relationship Between Sex-Role Stereotypes and Perceptions of the 'Good' Manager* Paper presented in partial fulfilment of the requirements for the Master of Business and Administration Degree, The Western Australian Institute of Technology, November

3   Radford, G. (1980) 'Women at the Top?' *Commonwealth Professional, No. 279,* (June), pp. 12–17

4   Powell, G.N. (1980) 'Career Development and the Woman Manager—A Social Power Perspective' *Personnel,* May–June, pp. 22–32

Chapter 6

1   Harragan, B.L. (1983) 'Women and Work: Jockeying for Position', in (ed.) *Jennie Farely: The Woman in Management: Career and Family Issues,* ILR Press: New York School of Industrial and Labor Relations, Cornell University, pp. 12–19

2   Baines, A. (1986) 'Women's Groups: Who Are They For?' *Women in Management Review, 2,* 2, (Summer), pp. 83–91

3   Still, L.V. and C. Guerin (1986) 'Networking Practices of Men and Women Managers Compared' *Women in Management Review, 2,* 2 (Summer), pp. 103–109

Chapter 9

1   Carland, J.W., F. Hoy, W.R. Boulton, and J.A. Carland (1984) 'Differentiating Entrepreneurs from Small Business Owners: A Conceptualisation' *Academy of Management Review, 9,* 2, pp. 354–359

2   Wojahn, E. (1986) 'Why Women's Business Does Not Turn Heads' *Business Review Weekly* 6 November, pp. 16–19

3   Goffee, R. and R. Scase (1985) *Women in Charge: The Experiences of Female Entrepreneurs* London: George Allen and Unwin

4   Bowen, D.D. and R.D. Hisrich (1986) 'The Female Entrepreneur: A Career Development Perspective' *Academy of Management Review, 11,* 2, pp. 393–407

Chapter 10

1   Highman, E.L. (1985) *The Organization Woman: Building a Career—An Inside Report* New York: Human Sciences Press Inc, pp. 12–13

Index

165

For Product Safety Concerns and Information please contact our EU
representative GPSR@taylorandfrancis.com Taylor & Francis Verlag GmbH,
Kaufingerstraße 24, 80331 München, Germany

Printed and bound by CPI Group (UK) Ltd, Croydon, CR0 4YY

08/05/2025

01864387-0004